Wolfgang Wickler

# The Marine Aquarium

*translated from the German by Gwynne Vevers*

Distributed in the U.S.A. by T.F.H. Publications, Inc., 211 West Sylvania Avenue, P.O. Box 27, Neptune City, N.J. 07753; in England by T.F.H. (Gt. Britain) Ltd., 13 Nutley Lane, Reigate, Surrey; in Canada by Clarke, Irwin & Company, Clarwin House, 791 St. Clair Avenue West, Toronto 10, Ontario; in Southeast Asia by Y. W. Ong, 9 Lorong 36 Geylang, Singapore 14; in Australia and the south Pacific by Pet Imports Pty. Ltd., P.O. Box 149, Brookvale 2100, N.S.W., Australia.
Published by T.F.H. Publications, Inc. Ltd., The British Crown Colony of Hong Kong.

131 line drawings by Hermann Kacher.

First published in Germany under the title *Das Meeresaquarium*.

© 1963 Frankh'sche Verlagshandlung, W. Keller & Co., Stuttgart
English translation © 1967 Studio Vista Limited

# Contents

Foreword                                                  7
What one cannot keep                                      8
Must it always be salt water?                             9
Salt-water fish and fresh-water fish                     11
  Do fish drink?                                          11
  Why are coralfish so brightly coloured?                12
  The habits of coralfish                                 13
Aquarists will swallow anything!                         15
Advice to the technically minded                         20
The sea water                                             21
The tank                                                  23
The installation                                          25
Aeration, lighting, filtration                           26
Plants                                                    28
Invertebrates in the marine aquarium                     30
The marine vivarium                                       37
Clever fish and stupid fish                              38
Fish wearing nighties                                    42
The coralfish community tank                             43
The food of coralfish                                    45
Some fish for the marine aquarium                        46
Alas, more unavoidable complications                     89
Can marine fish be bred?                                 91
A fish which mates with itself                           95
Biological specialities                                  97
The trade of cleaner                                    101
Some unfortunately common diseases                      105
Index                                                   109

# The Marine Aquarium

## Preface to the American Edition

For his work dealing with fish behavior, the explanations involved in making determinations of exactly how fishes behave and why they do the things they do, Dr. Wolfgang Wickler is almost without peer. The presentation of such behavioral information as it appears in *The Marine Aquarium* can be of special value to marine aquarists, because considerations of a fish's behavior are vitally concerned with the desirability of those actions in the aquarium.

On the other hand, the original English version of this book was in a small paperback edition, without a single illustration in color, and not even a photograph in black and white inside the book to illustrate the fishes to which the author referred. The original type was small, difficult to read and badly printed.

The scientific editors of TFH made a completely new edition of the book and prepared it for an American audience, only to be faced with a contract which forbade the alteration of the book without approval. In order to bring you this book and to make it as useful as possible, our alternative has been to ignore the taxonomic differences between those fish names denoted by Dr. Wickler and those in current usage, and to add color plates which have both the Wickler names and those names which we feel are more current.

In order to separate the responsibility of Dr. Wickler's original work from that of the TFH staff, we are using *in seratim* page numbers for the original text, and a series of "Color illustration" numbers to designate those color photographs which we have added. Thus, every color photo and its identification ⸳is solely the responsibility of TFH Publications, while everything that appears on a numbered page is the responsibility of the author.

The TFH Editors
1973

# Foreword

This volume is intended to be a report on our own experiences in running marine aquaria, rather than a textbook. In a textbook one can rightly expect to be presented with definite rules based on a series of comparable experiences, but this is scarcely possible today in the field of marine animals. We ourselves tried originally to keep our particular animals—tropical coralfish—in accordance with the advice given in published articles. In doing so we had to combine the instructions laid down by a number of different authors; one would say nothing about diet, while another would give no information on lighting or on the compatibility of the proposed inhabitants. However, we quickly gave up this method of making a collective assessment of the literature, because our first observations showed that the fish required something quite different. Since then we consult our animals, by altering their environment until they seem content. The criterion for this is that they should establish territories, form into pairs or in some cases begin to display and possibly spawn. Even with this method, however, the aquarist has to make a start somewhere, and so we first put the animals experimentally in an environment which appeared to us to be as close as possible to what we had observed in nature. This certainly seems sensible enough, but it does not always lead to success, because it is not possible to check on every point in the course of brief observations underwater. To observe the most important points the observer in the wild as well as the aquarist must have plenty of biological green fingers—or plenty of money.

It is to be hoped that this book will awaken the interest of the marine aquarist in some of the stimulating problems which can only be solved by patient and detailed observation in the aquarium. People are lavish in their praise of the beauty of coralfish, but the fish have something else to offer.

WOLFGANG WICKLER

# What one cannot keep

The living population of the sea consists of bacteria, algae, protozoans, sponges, coelenterates (jellyfish, sea-pens, corals, sea-anemones), a great number of worms (belonging to several zoological groups), a rich selection of large and small crustaceans (including barnacles), snails, bivalves, squid and octopus, bryozoans, arrow-worms, sea-stars, brittle-stars, feather-stars, sea-urchins, sea-cucumbers, sea-squirts, lancelets, hagfish and lampreys, sharks, rays and rabbit-fish, a very large number of bony fish, turtles, sea-snakes, sea-cows (manatee and dugong), dolphins and large whales. In theory all these belong in a marine aquarium, and if this is not a large enough selection the amphibians could be represented by the tadpoles of the Fire-bellied Toad which can be reared in brackish water.

However, the marine mammals are not suitable for our purpose on account of their size, unless one could fence in a sea bay, put in a dolphin and call it an aquarium. In fact the largest existing marine tank *is* something of this kind. This is at Marineland in Florida; it holds more than half a million gallons of water and is over 18 feet deep. Among other animals it houses 12-foot-long black Pilot Whales which each consume almost a hundredweight of squid a day.

The aquarist would have similar difficulties with many sharks, rays and large bony fish. But many smaller animals are also tricky; jellyfish, some crustaceans and cephalopods are particularly delicate, and bivalve molluscs, feather-stars and free-swimming plankton-feeders are difficult, at least where diet is concerned. With a few exceptions, the invertebrates can scarcely be kept successfully in the aquarium. Here we will only touch on them briefly, before turning our main attention to the fishes.

Even among the bony fishes there are many which cannot be kept in aquaria; these include those which are too large and the deep-sea forms which are extremely sensitive to light and particularly to small fluctuations in temperature (pressure plays a far less important part than one might think). Then there are the fish which are continuously on the move (and there are a great number of these) and the out-and-out specialists such as flying-fish, internal parasites (e.g. *Fierasfer* in sea-cucumbers) and so on.

From all this it might appear that there are very few animals left that are suitable for the marine aquarium. It is indeed true that the majority of the sea's inhabitants are unsuitable, but the remainder are still so numerous and varied that there will be no shortage of material for new discoveries now and in the future.

## Must it always be salt water?

This depends on your own wishes and those of your animals. One day a friend of mine decided to set up a marine aquarium: 'You see everyone has fresh-water tanks nowadays, there's nothing special in that!' There are several ways of satisfying the desire for something special. For instance, you could keep the small egg-laying toothcarp *Cyprinodon* or European sticklebacks in sea water. Naturally it would be somewhat odd to have Three-spined Sticklebacks swimming about in a coralfish tank. It is not uncommon for an aquarist to try keeping salt-water fish in fresh water because he is particularly interested in these animals but cannot afford to set up a sea-water tank. But anyone who keeps fresh-water fish in sea water creates quite a sensation. I would recommend him to use the following simpler method. Just set up a tank without plants but with sea sand, bivalve shells and corals, obtain some *Stigmatogobius* or a related fresh-water goby (e.g. *Proterorhinus* from Austria or *Gobius fluviatilis* from Lake Garda), the small fresh-water flatfish *Trinectes*, the Silverfish *Monodactylus*, a pair of blennies (*Blennius fluviatilis*) from Lake Garda, perhaps also some small fresh-water shrimps or mitten-crabs and put them all—provided they do not fight—into a tank which has been simply filled with ordinary fresh water. He can then become known as a successful marine aquarist and will have an additional thrill when he lets visitors taste his 'sea' water.

Sometimes dealers recommend fish that can be 'kept in brackish water', which is to be made by adding cooking salt to ordinary aquarium fresh water. This can in fact be done and the fish will live perfectly well. But brackish water must be hard, for soft brackish water gradually kills many fish. In nature, the brackish water zone occurs as a transition from salt to fresh water, and so varies considerably between ebb and flood tide. The fish, however, usually remain in their own home territory and so are washed by a succession of waters of varying salinities. Such fish are in fact relatively insensitive to fluctuations in salinity. The exact concentration of salt is not so important: water is said to be brackish when it has a salinity anywhere between 1 and 30 parts per thousand (normally expressed as $1^0/_{00}$ to $30^0/_{00}$). Nevertheless I would not recommend these fish to the beginner, because they tolerate and encourage inefficiency. (That is, some species do so, whereas others are delicate.) Furthermore they lead the aquarist, as he becomes more experienced, to reduce the amount of salt until finally the fish are swimming about in pure fresh water, and yet they still thrive. They would do the same in pure sea water, but this is not so easy to achieve. In the next chapter, I give some account of the physiological differences between fresh- and salt-water fish; brackish-water fish occupy an intermediate position for which they are specially adapted. For them, pure salt and pure fresh water are the extremes, in which they are, so to speak, balancing on the limits of their capabilities. It may be all right, but if there is a slight extra loading one way or the other the fish will probably succumb. As an example, let us take the well-known Indian cichlids in the genus *Etroplus*, of which both species, *E. maculatus* and *E. suratensis*, can be kept in pure fresh water. The smaller form *E. maculatus* will breed in this, but *E. suratensis* does not normally do so. From this it will be apparent that *E. maculatus* is better adapted to fresh water; nevertheless it has a tendency to become ill in pure fresh water. On the other hand, *E. suratensis* shows more brilliant coloration and will only breed with any ease when living in salty water, a sure sign that it is not so well adapted to fresh water, although it will grow in it. Furthermore it appears that acclimatization may play a part, because in India, where these fish are eaten, it is recognized that those originating in salty water settle down very badly in ponds, whereas fish caught in river mouths do so very well.

Coralfish require proper sea water. The aquarist wants a marine aquarium because it is still something of a novelty, and he wants coralfish because they are different. Exactly how different we shall now briefly describe.

# Salt-water fish and fresh-water fish

There are several differences between these two groups, which the ordinary fresh-water aquarist does not normally think about. In general, marine fish are no more difficult to keep than fresh-water fish, but they are certainly different. Unfortunately, it is more difficult to keep the sea water itself in the proper condition. However marine fish do have some peculiarities which will be obvious to anyone who keep his eyes open, and these can best be discussed by posing a few questions.

## Do fish drink?

The worst thing a ship-wrecked man can do is to drink sea water; even if his thirst is intolerable, this would only make it quite unbearable. But he can without hesitation squeeze a marine fish and drink the juice—a remarkable fact. In theory all fish in salt water should become desiccated, because the salt content of their body tissues is less than that of the sea. On purely physical grounds this would lead to an equilibrium, and since fish skin is permeable to water but not to salts, water would leave the body tissues. In this way the internal salt concentration would increase until it was as high as that outside—that is in theory. In practice, the body cells would have to give up so much water that they would become desiccated. Now if the fish simply drank water, it would certainly make good its water loss, but, as it only has salt water available, it would accumulate more and more salt within its body until it reached equilibrium with the surrounding water. At any rate this is what the common mussel and the lugworm *Arenicola* can do. However, the metabolic processes of a fish are differently adjusted and they do not tolerate so much salt. But because the fish loses water automatically and can only replace it by drinking salt water it must in some way get rid of the excess salt, and this it does mainly through the gills. By this means it keeps the *status quo*: it loses more water, drinks and then excretes the excess salt and in so doing uses up a great amount of energy. As one can see this is a very complicated process. It could be much simpler, as is shown by the algae or the common mussel. But fish have not evolved only for salt water; they have merely become modified to deal with it, and this does not lead to an ideal solution.

In fresh-water fish the position is exactly the reverse. Their bodies contain more salt than the water around them, and so water is constantly entering through the skin, in order to dilute this salt content. Fresh-water fish do not therefore need to drink; on the contrary they would swell and finally burst if they did not continuously excrete the invading water in the urine. This, at least, is something salt-water fish are spared.

Fish which migrate from fresh to sea water are particularly adaptable, and so are brackish-water fish which have to be capable of dealing with both fresh and salt water (cf. p. 11).

*Why are coralfish so brightly coloured?*

Aquarists may be forgiven if they place the coralfish first among the inhabitants of their marine tanks. Naturally some marine fish are less brightly coloured and some are quite drab: fish on sandy bottoms are sand-coloured, those in open water are dark above—being brown, blue or greenish according to the colour of the water in which they live—and silvery below, so that they appear like the water surface when seen from below. At first sight these fish appear unicoloured, but closer examination shows something different. They have to conceal themselves from enemies in their monotone environment, but not from their mates. So they make special signals; they may, for example, suddenly unfold strikingly coloured fins (usually the first dorsal) which are normally hidden, or the whole body or part of it may assume a contrasting pattern for a short time.

On the other hand most coralfish are brilliantly coloured the whole time. At first the term coralfish was used for all small fish which occur constantly or occasionally on coral-reefs. The term soon became associated with any very brightly coloured fish, so that nowadays it is not unusual for any brilliantly coloured marine fish to be known as 'coralfish'. Many workers have tried to discover why they are so brightly coloured. But usually they have made the mistake of trying to explain the coloration of a single species or even the patterns of coralfish in general. In fact one must proceed step by step, because it is quite normal for colour elements with quite different functions to be combined in the same fish. The very common black band on the head camouflages the eyes—but from whom? Hitherto we only knew that *Runula* (see page 83) attacked the eyes of other fish. The eye masking is therefore a piece of camouflage coloration. But this certainly does not apply to the conspicuous eye-spot which is frequently positioned somewhere on the hind part of the body. We do not know its function. According to the older literature, *Chaetodon capistratus* (see plate III, 11) was said to swim slowly backwards and deceive its enemy by unexpectedly rushing off very much faster in the opposite direction. We have not seen this either in this or in any other fish with an eye-spot, nor have we found any eye-witness of such behaviour.

Camouflage coloration is less common among peaceful fish which have territories and hiding-places in the reef than it is among those which position themselves in groups above the reef or wander far and wide for their food (*Haemulon, Heniochus*). Naturally enough predators (*Epinephelus, Cephalopholis, Scorpaena*) which lie in wait for prey are difficult to see. One must, however, avoid drawing false conclusions from observations made in the aquarium: some fish which are very conspicuous in a tank may be almost invisible in the open water owing to the play of waves and shafts of sunlight on the irregular background. The opposite is the case with the Banded Puller, *Dascyllus aruanus* (plate VI, 6) which is often cited as a good example of colour camouflage that breaks up the outline of the body. In the aquarium it is often difficult to discern among white coral branches. In nature, on the other hand, it lives in among brightly coloured branches of living coral and its black and white dress is then very striking—and probably acts as a species recognition signal.

Indeed it is likely that many of the characteristic brightly coloured coralfish patterns do in fact serve in species recognition. With so many species living in close proximity, there must be some means of finding the correct partner. The juvenile coloration of many species (*Coris formosa*, plate VII, 5; Imperial Angelfish, plate IV, 2; Sweetlips, plate I, 13) is often very different from that of the adults, because the young move about in another milieu and in other company.

## The habits of coralfish

I know that this heading is not particularly clear, but I hope the reader will understand what is intended.

Coralfish are not only more brightly coloured than fresh-water fish but on the average they are also more active. There are some fresh-water fish which are as brightly coloured and active but there are not so many of them. Anyone who keeps coralfish will not only see more movement and more colour but also many examples of extreme specialization. He will find more interesting associations between quite unrelated fish (see p. 97). On the other hand, he will have less opportunity of observing a highly developed family life. Many marine fish have pelagic eggs that drift freely and untended in the open water. As might be expected this almost never happens among fresh-water fish because the eggs would all too easily be washed ashore on the nearest bank. It is true that among marine fish there are mouth-brooders (*Apogon*, some catfishes) and pouch-breeders (sea-horses) which guard the eggs, but they do not look after the larvae. This also applies to the Pomacentridae which are closely related to the cichlids: *Amphiprion* species form permanent pairs which guard the spawn laid on a rock in the same way as many cichlids, but the larvae simply swim up towards the light—that is to the water surface (see p. 93).

Indeed one must first discover what it is that is so worthwhile observing in marine fish. Some of the more recent discoveries are discussed in the section on biological specialities (p. 97), and these suggest that there are still many new and exciting things to be found out.

# Aquarists will swallow anything!

An aquarium is a spatial structure whose capacity can be calculated according to the formula: length × breadth × height, expressed in cubic centimetres, cubic inches, gallons or some other unit measurement. If such a tank has sides of equal length it will be a cube. In recent aquarium literature I have frequently found the statement: 'this fish is best kept in a "metre tank"'. Evidently the readers have all quite surprisingly swallowed this 'metre tank' because I have heard no shouts of protest. Correctly speaking this would mean a cube-shaped tank, each side 100 cm. (about 39 inches) long, which would hold a cubic metre of water. This appears to me to be somewhat massive for a modern living-room. And if only one side were 100 cm. long, how long would the other sides be and how much water would the tank contain?

This is just one example of how inexact many such instructions are. Indeed at the present time the keeping of marine aquaria is suffering from the fact that only occasionally does one find really workable data, formulae, etc. In spite of its history over about fifty years, this hobby is still so new that every printed statement is treated with profound respect: personal experience which might raise doubts is still too often lacking. There is, in fact, every reason to scrutinize most carefully what you read in the literature and not to believe everything that is dished up.

For example, in 1956 a guide to the care and breeding of all species of sea-horses was published. We are not concerned here with the title of the book or the name of the author. The courtship and mating and the birth of the young sea-horses was shown in twelve large photographs. These enlargements looked inspiring, but there were many points which did not agree with what we know about European sea-horses from the work of K. Fiedler (1955, *Zeitschrift für Tierpsychologie*, vol. 11, pp. 358–416). Here I have put Fiedler's statements and illustrations alongside those of the other author; under (*a*) is given the caption printed under the picture in the other author's first book, under (*b*) is the caption printed under the same photograph in another book published in the same year (1956) by the same author:

Fig. 1.

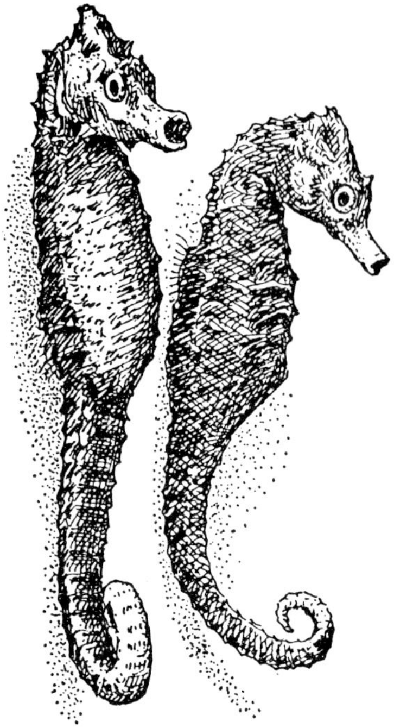

Fig. 2.

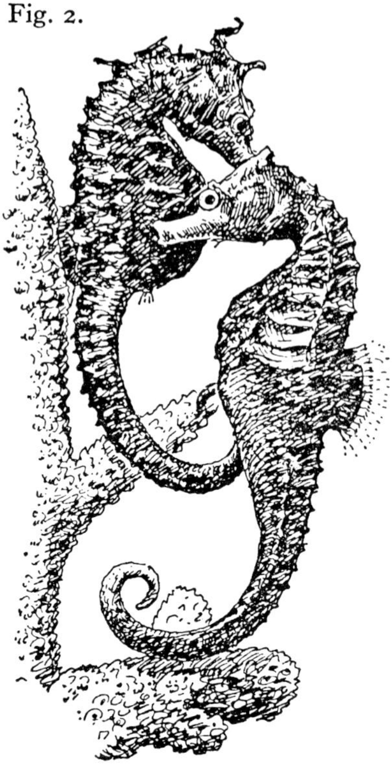

Fig. 3.

1. (*a*) The pair begin courtship (fig. 1).
   (*b*) Sea-horse pair. The male (left) is swollen by the developing young.
2. (*a*) The courting fish face one another (fig. 2).
   (*b*) Mating begins when the female approaches the male from the front.
3. (*a*) If you look carefully, you can see the female's ovipositor penetrating the male (fig. 3).
   (*b*) This beautiful photograph shows how the female sea-horse (right) inserts its ovipositor into the brood-pouch of the male.

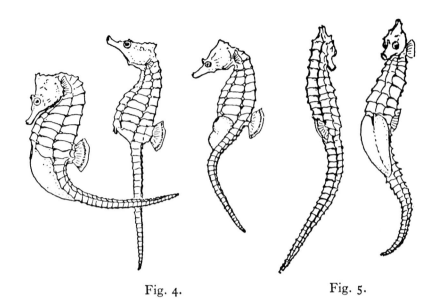

Fig. 4.

Fig. 5.

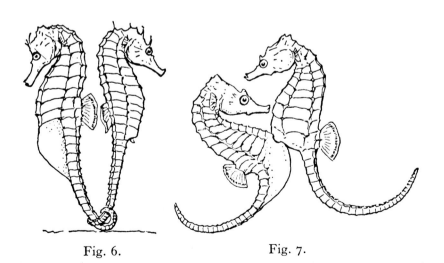

Fig. 6.

Fig. 7.

18

4. Fish ready to mate swim with the head pressed down (left) and the tail trailing behind along the substrate. The males also 'pump', that is, they bend the tail forwards and thus compress the brood-pouch. The rather more excited female quickly lifts its head and in so doing may swim a little bit upwards (fig. 4).

5. Swimming, as though round a maypole, the pair rise to the surface (fig. 5). (This remarkable and attractive behaviour has been known for about forty years!)

6. In *Hippocampus guttulatus* the pair then link tails, facing away from each other, and sink, sometimes right to the bottom (fig. 6). Then they begin to circle round again.

7. During the transfer of the eggs the fish swim free in the water and hold their tails bent away from each other (fig. 7).

From the other author's first caption it appears that the male in the first photograph is courting, but according to the alternative caption he is already carrying young. Furthermore, in the third picture, in spite of the caption, the male is obviously the fish on the right, recognizable by the brood-pouch which fills the embayment between belly and tail.

Apart from the text there are various remarkable points concerning the photographs themselves: in the first picture both fish are holding their mouths wide open, which they normally never do; they remain on coral branches while mating, which again they never do under normal circumstances; in all the photographs the tails are coiled away from the substrate, which is almost impossible physiologically, for the prehensile tail will only bend towards an object that it touches, even if severed from the fish; the eyes lie very deep in the sockets while the fins and skin processes are in peculiar positions. It is particularly remarkable that the fish all show reflections, which do not appear in the water. From all this it is evident that the whole of the courtship and mating (and also the birth of the young which is not shown here) have been photographed in air from above using dead, dried sea-horses and pieces of coral on glass plates. The climax is the last picture (which I also found reproduced in *Tropical Fish Hobbyist* for October 1959); alongside all the mistakes already mentioned the ovipositor is pointing towards the left-hand fish, so it must come from the right-hand fish, but the latter is a male and has no ovipositor. By now the suspicious observer will very quickly recognize that the ovipositor is a needle! The whole series of photographs is a complete fraud, but many will be deceived.

As you see Fiedler's simple line drawings (reproduced directly from the originals) are far more accurate than the photographs which Herr Kacher has copied as faithfully as possible. Other photographic tricks include the use of Color Food which changes the colour of the fish's body, and the photography of dead fish laid out on a glass plate with fins spread, and taken against a particularly contrasting background. From all this, the aquarist can and must learn to keep his eyes open and to doubt as soon as the biological feeling is false. For it is evident that only a critical readership will force the necessary accuracy in published accounts and thus raise the level of aquarium literature, and also, as experience shows, make such writings of interest to the scientist.

## Advice to the technically minded

If you want to set up a marine aquarium it is best not to study a chemistry textbook nor to make a point of finding the most expensive accessories. For normal working you need no more than a watertight tank, the solution of salts given in the following section, a hydrometer, some aeration, a few rocks, adequate illumination, a filter with nylon wool (the filter is superfluous most of the time in tanks containing only invertebrates) and—for tropical animals—controlled heating. You cannot use special apparatus to replace the care and attention with which you must watch over this living environment. Finally, in my opinion, it is high time that the aquarium accessories marketed—whether air taps, pumps or filter media—were tested just as critically as cameras or diving watches.

# The sea water

Aquaria, and particularly public aquaria, that are situated close to the sea usually pump natural sea water through their tanks: this is known as the open system. On progressive, civilized coasts, however, the water is often so dirty that neither fish nor public can tolerate it. In such places the sea water must be cleansed before use, and the system used will then be closed or semi-closed. The aquarist living inland can only use a closed circulation and usually his sea water has to be artificial. He could, of course, fetch his own natural sea water, as for example the Schönbrunn Aquarium in Vienna does in its own tanker lorries; with large volumes of sea water this might well be cheaper—but then how many of us have a tanker lorry?

Artificial sea water can be prepared according to the Wiedermann–Kramer formula, using distilled water as a basis; in industrial areas rain water is too dirty, and besides in most places it runs through tarred or galvanized gutters. The most suitable place for an aquarist's house would be close to a mountain water supply, for there he could use tap water direct.

The formula for artificial sea water is as follows:

In 100 litres of distilled water dissolve:

2765 g. NaCl (iodine-free cooking salt)
692 g. $MgSO_4 \cdot 7H_2O$ (crystalline magnesium sulphate)
551 g. $MgCl_2 \cdot 6H_2O$ (crystalline magnesium chloride)
65 g. KCl (potassium chloride)
25 g. $NaHCO_3$ (sodium bicarbonate)
10 g. NaBr (sodium bromide)
5 g. $Na_2HPO_4$ (sodium phosphate)
1·5 g. $SrCl_2$ (strontium chloride)
0·5 g. KI (potassium iodide)

About 1 litre of the 100 litres should be kept aside and used to dissolve 145 g. $CaCl_2 \cdot 6H_2O$ (crystalline calcium chloride). This should only be added to the main solution when all the other ingredients have been dissolved.

In aquarium tanks the water soon becomes enriched with nitrates derived from the remains of food and from the animals' excretions, and there is no really practical method of removing these compounds. Good filter charcoal does indeed adsorb some of them, but the more expensive charcoal which we now buy neither does this nor in general adsorbs anything, not even trypaflavin. The only efficient and reliable means of dealing with poisonous nitrate present in high concentration is to replace a proportion of the old sea water with new. Therefore it is senseless to add to the new water the sodium nitrate which is mentioned in formulae for a sea water that is as close as possible to natural sea water; one simply leaves it out. It is only in the case of marine plants grown alone, that is in tanks without animals, that one adds 10 g. sodium nitrate to the formula given above (cf. the formula for algal fertilizer, p. 29).

If necessary, sea water can be made up and stored at five times concentration (dissolve the above mentioned quantities of salts in 20 litres of water; the calcium chloride should be kept separately in dissolved or crystalline form).

Before use, the freshly prepared water should be vigorously aerated for several hours, or preferably days, in order to drive off the excess of chlorine which is usually present (but on this see also p. 105).

There is some doubt about when the nitrate becomes poisonous, but it is supposedly when the concentration exceeds 100 mg. per litre. The highest concentration I have so far measured in an aquarist's tank was 900 to 1100 mg. per litre, and yet the tank contained completely healthy coralfish. My own sea water usually has about 500 mg. per litre, and even newly introduced fish appear to thrive in this—so far as one can judge.

The pH of the sea water can be raised with sodium bicarbonate or lowered with phosphoric acid, so that it stands at 8·2–8·6; the extreme permissible limits are 7·5 and 9·5.

For fish from tropical regions the water should be kept at a temperature of 22–28°C (72–82°F), for those from the Mediterranean at 22–25°C (72–77°F) and for North Temperate fish and invertebrates at about 15–19°C (59–66°F).

In nature, the density (specific gravity) and the salinity of the water fluctuate from place to place and even in the same place at different times. So it is not possible to specify a normal density for sea water. However most animals are not sensitive to slow fluctuations in density, which occur unavoidably as a result of evaporation and topping up with distilled water. Some fish are not affected at all when they are suddenly moved into water of a different density—they only breathe a little more vigorously for a while. Occasionally they may be a little too heavy or too light, according to whether they have come from lighter or heavier sea water, but in either case they quite quickly adjust themselves. The water is usually kept at a density of 1027, but so far none of my animals have suffered damage at densities of 1017 or 1033. A hydrometer is used to check the density which is read off at the point where the water surface cuts across the hydrometer scale.

It is important not to confuse the density and the salinity. The salinity is expressed in parts per thousand, e.g. $34^0/_{00}$. The density is expressed as e.g. 1025, 1027, etc., or sometimes as 25, 27, the first two figures, which are constant, being omitted. From my own experience, I know that some readers easily change 'salinity 34' into 'density 34'. A density of 1027 corresponds to a salinity of 34·52%. The density can easily be converted into salinity (or vice versa) by using the following formulae, in which $S$ denotes the salinity in $^0/_{00}$, $\sigma_0$ the density (e.g. 1027), $\sigma_+$ the last two figures of $\sigma_0$ (more exactly: one takes the specific gravity of water as 1000, and denotes by $\sigma_+$ the amount by which the sea water is heavier, i.e. 1027 minus 1000 = 27).

Formula I:

$$S = 0.03 + 1.805 \frac{1.1 + \sigma_+}{1.47}$$

When the salinity $S$ is known, one first finds the value of $S_+$ and from this derives the density $\sigma_0$.

Formula II:

$$\sigma_+ = 1.47 \frac{S - 0.03}{1.805} - 1.1$$

## The tank

A marine tank should have a capacity of at least 7 gallons; such a tank could accommodate four $2\frac{1}{2}$-inch *Dascyllus trimaculatus*. Nevertheless I would not recommend a capacity of less than 20 gallons for marine fish. From the biological viewpoint there is no upper limit to the size of the tank. The smaller the amount of water available for each fish, the more difficult will be the task of maintenance, and the more one will have to filter, aerate and renew the water.

The sea water ought never to come into contact with metal. Air taps and clamps of brass, which dangle in the water and produce verdigris are particularly dangerous. There are so many methods of painting the tank itself that it is scarcely possible to enumerate them all. The simplest method is to buy a ready-made asbestos cement tank; a fire-enamelled angle-iron tank is also clean and cheap; for complete reliability, but at greater cost one can have a tank made of polyvinyl chloride (PVC) or of timber and asbestos cement painted inside with epoxy resin.

The glass panes are usually fixed in with a mastic containing no lead. Prestik mastic which always remains soft is physiologically unobjectionable, but it gradually oozes out along the outer sides of the panes and quickly crumbles in sea water. The panes should therefore be cut to fit as closely as possible so that only a very narrow groove remains. Experience with sealing compounds for filling up the grooves is very conflicting. In spite of many doubts, some experiments in which the panes were simply cemented to the tank frame with a stiff epoxy resin have been very encouraging. Another method, which is cleaner than mastic, is to set the panes in a carefully constructed groove in the frame. The groove is wide enough to accommodate the thickness of the glass and also a length of plastic tubing (external to the glass) which becomes squeezed by the water pressure and effectively seals the tank. For fixing panes $\frac{1}{4}$ inch thick we have a groove $\frac{3}{8}$ inch wide and use plastic tubing with an external diameter of $\frac{1}{8}$ inch; in practice we use three pieces of such tubing running round alongside each other. Unlike rubber, the plastic tubing does not become slimy.

As most fish will at times jump out of the tank—even boxfish when they are scared—it is essential to have a good tank cover. It is customary to use glass sheets for this purpose (see in the section on lighting for the disadvantages). When it evaporates sea water leaves behind salt, which is very hygroscopic, so the cover glasses must be cleaned regularly and care should be taken to see that salt water does not drip on to furniture.

# The installation

Almost all coral-reef fish require hiding-places; the only exceptions are the typical free-swimming forms such as the Carangidae. Others —*Platax, Monodactylus*—are content with a simple division of the space. It is usual to set up groups of corals in the tank. These are the dead, mostly bleached calcareous skeletons, and they show numerous pores from which the living coral animals protrude their tentacle crowns which are usually coloured. Dead pieces of coral polyp often remain inside the coral and these will foul the water in a very short time. For this reason the corals should be steeped for some days in dilute sodium hydroxide and then very thoroughly washed.

Coral pieces have one advantage: they look attractive, particularly when algae start to settle on them. But they have their disadvantages: things get caught up in them, they are brittle and heavy to handle, and their sharp edges will tear any net in quite a short time. They are not dangerous to the fish.

It will be necessary to catch up fish if they become ill or if one of them develops into a bully. To do this, however, necessitates clearing out the whole tank—the beginner may find he has to do this quite often. This job is much easier to do if the tank is decorated with rocks or upright and horizontal flat sheets of gneiss, from which good crevices and caves can be constructed. Bottom-living fish, including many blennies, live under half flowerpots or similar objects, tube-dwellers will make a home, according to their size, in empty snail shells or pieces of plastic tubing; in the latter case one end should be sealed off. Surgeonfish and soldierfish require plenty of free space for swimming. The Pomacanthidae, Chaetodontidae, wrasse, grunts and others require hiding-places as well as free swimming space.

The easiest tanks to keep clean are those which do not have a sandy bottom. This type of tank would be very good for the species of *Amphiprion* and *Dascyllus*. If necessary, the ugly bottom of the tank can be hidden with a thin layer of coarse gravel. Anyone who likes sand or who requires it for sand-dwelling fauna (gobies, flatfish, many wrasse and particularly invertebrates) should use genuine fine-grained sea sand and not coarse gravel, which does not suit the sand-dwellers. The substrate can safely contain calcareous stones, because calcium is a normal constituent of sea water.

25

# Aeration, lighting, filtration

The aeration should produce bubbles that are as small as possible (diameter less than 1 mm.). The easiest way to achieve this is with a piece of beech or lime wood, used in the same way as a purchased diffuser. Pure oxygen can sometimes be used as a substitute, but it must then be in large bubbles; very small oxygen bubbles are extremely poisonous to the fish. It is not advisable to aerate with air from a room which contains tobacco smoke.

Many animals enjoy the water movements produced by aeration; in cases where they are disturbed by it, aeration can be carried out in the filter or in a partitioned corner of the tank just before the outlet to the filter.

The fish should only show quite small respiratory movements of the mouth and gill-covers; in no circumstance should they gasp or hang at the surface. There is no need to worry that the filtration or even strong aeration will overstimulate the sense organs of the fish or cause them to undertake too much manoeuvring, for compared with the noise and turbulence of the swell on a seaward reef the aquarist produces little more than a gentle murmur.

In general, marine aquaria require more light than fresh-water tanks. The green algae will only grow in very strong light, and the fish, which are accustomed to brilliant sunlight on the tropical reefs, may even assume their nocturnal coloration during the day, if they are kept in tanks that are too dark. A 20-gallon tank requires two 40-watt fluorescent tubes, and it is recommended that one tube should be bluish and the other yellowish. Many aquarists also use ultraviolet light (UV), which at the same time kills bacteria, but it only penetrates a short distance into water. Fish which continually or at times swim at the surface or those which have parts of the body or fins sticking out above the surface should be protected from UV light, otherwise they will quickly become sunburnt. Ordinary glass sheets filter almost all the UV component from the light, and so tanks illuminated with blue or ultraviolet light must be covered with some other material. The best thing to use is nylon or terylene netting with a mesh small enough to prevent the fish jumping through it.

Some fish panic when the lights are turned off suddenly in the evening. So it is a good idea, particularly with newly imported fish, to give them a little twilight. This can easily be done by turning off the tank lights and letting the room lights burn for a further twenty to thirty minutes.

Dirty, cloudy sea water is worse for fish than unclean fresh water. So marine tanks require plenty of filtration. We filter only through nylon wool, occasionally using activated charcoal as a substitute. The nylon should be regularly washed out and it can then be used again. For large tanks (over 200 gallons) a normal sand or grit filter is more suitable. Very clear water can be obtained if the rate of filtration is high and this can be achieved by the use of a circulation pump; naturally the pumps must be watertight, and they are best made of plastic. Of course, with this method plankton organisms will quickly be removed, unless they are retained by algal growths in the tank or by dense decorative effects. In order to preserve the plankton one can use a sand filter with a large surface area, through which the water only flows at a slow rate. But this is scarcely practicable for the average aquarist. The filtered water should be led to the bottom of the tank. The outgoing water can simply overflow through an outlet and into the filter which is at about the same level. The heater can also be put in the filter where it will not be in the way and where it can never become dry if the pump fails. The heated water enters the tank at the bottom, rises to the surface and thus brings the whole tank to the same temperature. Some success has also been achieved with the installation of a second sieve in the form of a perforated plate at the bottom of the tank. This plate (of plastic) is first covered with nylon gauze and then with the sea sand. The filter water is led in under the double bottom, so that it must pass through the sand which is thus always kept clean. In crevices and under stones where the fish like to dig hiding-places and where food remains sometimes accumulate, the layer of sand will be thinner and there the through current will be at its strongest; in this way these dirty corners will automatically be swept clean. This method can also be used in fresh-water tanks, but then the plants will grow very badly because their roots are continuously being washed from below.

Internal filters are not recommended because they have a poor performance and are difficult to clean. Even an external filter only collects the dirt into an easily accessible place, it does not remove it from the circulation and so a filter of this type must be frequently cleaned.

In this account I have only written of what we ourselves have tried. The experience of others with various filter media and further technical advice will be found in the *Proceedings of the International Congress of Aquariology* (Monaco, 1962).

# Plants

Marine aquaria usually have no plants, or if they do, only a few. The only plants we are concerned with here are various species of algae. It is quite usual for a coating of blue-green algae (Cyanophyceae) of various colours to appear. If this becomes too thick (as a rule this indicates that the tank is being kept too dark), it should be removed, otherwise it will quickly spread and cover the sand and this will discourage animals from burrowing. It is even worse when this alga suddenly dies and fouls all the water. This also applies to the mats of filamentous green algae which (with more powerful illumination) often grow on rocks and corals in marine tanks. These mats should be dealt with quite regularly by removing the rocks and giving them a thorough brush. If the algae are allowed to die in the tank as they may do with copper sulphate treatment (see p. 107) they will cause mass mortality among the fish.

So far the only plants that can be recommended are a few green

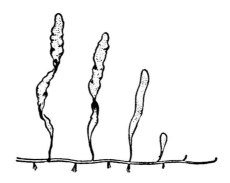

Fig. 8. The green alga *Caulerpa*

algae in the genus *Caulerpa*: *C. fasciata* is found on the coasts of Europe, while *C. prolifera*, *C. crassifolia* and *C. sertularioides* come from Florida. They grow a stock which creeps through the sand, every now and again giving off colourless rhizoids below and large, leaf-like thalli above (fig. 8). These algae require as much light as possible.

The following nutrient solutions can be used as algal fertilizers:

1. 1 litre water

   20 g. $NaNO_3$* (sodium nitrate)
   20 g. $KNO_3$* (potassium nitrate)
   10 g. $NH_4NO_3$ (ammonium nitrate), with traces of potassium bromide and potassium iodide.

2. 800 cc. water

   40 g. $NaHPO_4$ (sodium phosphate)
   40 g. $CaCl_2$ (crystalline calcium chloride)
   20 g. $FeCl_3$ (ferric chloride)
   20 g. HCL (concentrated hydrochloric acid)

For green algae one should use 1 cc. of solution per litre of tank water every five days. The salts marked with an *asterisk* (*) should be omitted if the tank is also occupied by animals. However, we ourselves have so far been quite successful without using these nutrient solutions.

Algae are sensitive to changes in density.

# Invertebrates in the marine aquarium

We have had quite a number of invertebrate animals in our marine tanks, although rather few of these were intentional. In an aquarium that is maintained correctly from the biological viewpoint, various small invertebrates (e.g. tiny crustaceans, such as harpacticids) will establish themselves, and usually some larger ones will soon appear; this process can be helped by the occasional introduction into the tank of some living seaweed or a few stones with an algal covering.

Fig. 9. A tubeworm

All sorts of animals will emerge from these, but of course they will be an easy prey for prowling predatory fish. Small sponges or sea-squirts will be fairly safe as they mostly remain completely hidden. In general, it is best to keep invertebrates alone, without fish; this is technically easier and—with a few exceptions—it suits the invertebrates better.

Fig. 10. A king-crab

Here I would like to mention a few invertebrate forms which we have kept successfully.

## Sponges

Many small sponges will do well in the aquarium provided they are undamaged. They all require plenty of oxygen. They feed on very finely particulate food which usually develops naturally in old tanks that are left fallow. The greyish-yellow to vermilion sponge *Suberites domuncula* is common in the Mediterranean and parts of western Europe; it often lives on the 'houses' of hermit-crabs and reaches a diameter of up to 7 inches.

Sponges do not tolerate the sting-cell poison of sea-anemones.

## Coelenterates

In the aquarium, colonies of tiny hydroid polyps frequently grow on all kinds of hard objects. In nature some of the best known are *Sertularia* and *Tubularia*, and also the velvety-white or pink *Hydractinia echinata* which covers the 'houses' of hermit-crabs—specimens imported with tropical material are often difficult to identify. These hydroids feed on tiny plankton organisms.

In our tanks we repeatedly have tiny free-swimming medusae, which Dr Werner (Heligoland) has identified as *Cladonema mayeri* Perkins (known from Tortugas and California). The polyp stages, from which the medusae are produced, grow as a network on the tank walls and on parts of the glass. They are not fed specially, but the medusae always appear at regular intervals.

It is possible to keep pieces of true coral for quite a long time in an aquarium with clear water, but this is a rather specialized task for the advanced aquarist. The polyps, which are usually very brightly coloured, extend their tentacles from the calcareous skeletons and catch tiny invertebrates; they will also take *Tubifex*, which they pass into the mouth in slow motion, like long noodles.

Various sea-anemones (Actiniaria) can be kept successfully in aquaria. Some of the largest species with a diameter of $4\frac{1}{2}$ feet belong to the genus *Stoichactis*; they are used as homes by anemone-fish (*Amphiprion*, see p. 69). These giant anemones can live for more than sixty years, but in the aquarium they usually die back after a certain time. Some species are sensitive to red and infra-red light. All actinians like clear water, rich in oxygen, and suffer considerably if overfed. They will then contract quite quickly into small, bedraggled lumps of jelly, but will soon expand again. They should only be fed if they show, by the extension of the tentacles, that they are hungry. Usually they pick up sufficient food from the general feeding in the tank. It is an advantage to add Vitamin T and nicotinamide as a supplement to the food. Giant anemones will take *Tubifex* with their tentacle tips.

Apart from the giant anemones, many aquarists keep the variably coloured opelet anemone (*Anemonia sulcata*) from shallow water on rocky coasts, the very hardy beadlet anemone (*Actinia equina*) which is a deep red, the wartlet anemone (*Bunodactis verrucosa*) and a few others. These sea-anemones should all be fed twice a week with small pieces of mussel flesh, earthworms, or with *Daphnia, Cyclops* and *Tubifex*. They and the giant actinians do better without fish in the tank.

The various species of *Aiptaisia* will grow and breed if they too are fed sparingly; like *Bunodactis* and *Actinia equina*, they are viviparous, that is, the young spend the larval stage in the body cavity of the mother, who spits them out as fully formed young when they have reached the twelve-tentacle stage.

The vestlet anemones (*Cerianthus*) are more delicate. They build deep, curved tubes with walls reinforced with mucus, in sandy and muddy substrates. They and some of the tubeworms (see below) do not attain their full size and beauty until it is dark, for this is the time when many small crustaceans, for which they lie in wait, start to leave their hiding-places in the bottom.

## Snails

Some of the Chitons or coat-of-mail shells also last for quite a time without any special care. These are about an inch long and have a creeping foot like the true snails. Instead of a coiled shell they have an elongate oval shell made up of eight segments; from above they look rather like water-slaters.

Of the true snails or gastropods, the easiest to keep are the predators. For instance, the species of *Murex* from the Mediterranean, which every now and again require a living mussel, or the cone-shells (*Conus*) which eat fish flesh and have an extremely poisonous stiletto with which they kill sleeping fish on the bottom at night-time. The Netted Dog-whelk, *Nassa reticulata*, which is about 1 inch long, is very useful as a consumer of food remains, but it apparently does not survive temperatures above 25°C (77°F).

The cowries (*Cypraea*) which will eat flesh as well as algae also do well. The remarkable worm-snails (*Vermetus*) live in vertical tubular shells, rather like the tubeworms, and catch tiny animals with long lassoes of mucus.

Particularly attractive are the nudibranch snails which carry no shell, but have filamentous, tubular or tree-like processes on the body which are actually gills; they feed on hydrozoans, bryozoans, sponges and similar, and so they are difficult to keep. On the other hand there are small, quite drably coloured, relatives of the sea-hare (*Aplysia*) which last well and reproduce freely; they have a thin horny shell which is almost completely covered by the two halves of the mantle which meet dorsally. They eat only algae; when disturbed some of them expel clouds of coloured secretion.

### Bivalve molluscs

These do not last very well in the aquarium. Examples are the cockles (*Cardium*), the 3-inch-long *Arca noae* and the fan-shell (*Pinna*) which have been kept for up to six months. They should be fed with coarse plankton.

### Cephalopods

This is the mollusc group which contains the octopuses, squids and cuttlefishes. The common octopus of the Mediterranean or similar species elsewhere is suitable for the marine aquarium, but only so long as it remains small, because when fully grown it has an arm span of 8–9 feet. The lesser octopus (*Eledone moschata*) which also occurs in the Mediterranean and along parts of the coasts of western Europe can also be kept; it has only a single row of suckers on the arms.

An octopus should be kept by itself, for in a short time it will catch all the fish. It will also eat crustaceans, particularly medium-sized shore-crabs.

Color illustration 1. *Spirographis spallanzani*, a sabellid tube worm.

Color illustration 2. *Anemonia sulcata,* opelet anemone. Photo by U. Erich Friese.

Color illustration 3. *Cerianthus,* vestlet anemone or cylinder sea anemone.

Color illustration 4. *Pagurus prideauxi (Eupagurus prideauxi),* European hermit crab, with the sea anemone *Adamsia* attached to its shell. Photo by U. Erich Friese.

Octopus show an astonishing range of colour change, depending upon their mood. They are highly intelligent, and their tank must have a close-fitting lid as they can squeeze through extremely small slits.

## Annelid worms

This is the group to which the earthworms, whiteworms, *Tubifex* and leeches belong. Some of their marine relatives can be kept in the aquarium, where they mostly live hidden in the substrate or under stones. Others, however, are quite conspicuous, particularly the tubeworms in the families Sabellidae (e.g. *Spirographis*) and Serpulidae. These live in self-made tubes which are sometimes horny, sometimes mucilaginous; the tubes protrude vertically from the sand or mud. The striking crown of delicate, feathered tentacles emerges from the top of the tube and waves gently back and forwards as the worm feeds on tiny organisms. If, however, the worm is disturbed in any way the tentacles are very rapidly withdrawn into the tube.

## King-crabs

The king-crabs or Xiphosura are not crustaceans but primitive relations of the spiders and scorpions. The best known genus is *Limulus*. They come from the coasts of south-east Asia and the northwest Atlantic, and feed on worms, small bivalves, dead fish and similar. The conspicuous, non-movable eyes are positioned high up on the horseshoe-shaped carapace. They do well and live for quite a time at a temperature of about 20°C (71°F). One species grows to a length of 18 inches or more.

King-crabs should be fed every second day and this is best done according to Professor Kuhn's method (especially if they are being kept in a small tank where they can easily be reached). The animal is laid upside down on the edge of the tank or on any flat surface and a clump of *Tubifex* is placed between its legs. It will start to feed immediately. After the meal the king-crab is rinsed and returned to the tank. This ensures that it always receives fresh food, one is easily able to add vitamins, and see which animal is satisfied and which will not feed. And finally the tank remains completely free of food remains.

## Crustaceans

Certain crustaceans (*Artemia*, shrimps, prawns, small crabs) are used as food in the marine aquarium. Tropical hermit-crabs are sometimes kept and they are valuable as consumers of food remains. However, they do not usually last long if they should happen to moult, for then they are easily killed by their companions and one is left with nothing but a number of large empty snail shells. The European hermit-crab *Eupagurus prideauxi*, which carries the sea-anemone *Adamsia* on its shell, does very badly in aquaria.

The prawn *Stenopus hispidus* is often imported from the West Indies. It is about $3\frac{1}{2}$ inches long and has striking red and white rings round the body and round the third pair of thoracic legs (pincers) which are about the length of the body. Its white antennae are even longer. In my experience these prawns will feed on various small animals, such as *Gammarus*, *Tubifex* and midge larvae. But they also clean fish (see page 100), and so are called barber-shop shrimps. They are rather aggressive so it is best to keep only one in a tank. In the wild they live in pairs in siliceous sponges.

Some of the Mediterranean prawns are suitable as consumers of food remains, e.g. *Lysmata seticaudata* ($2\frac{1}{2}$ inches) or *Leander serratus* which is also common in north-west Europe. In all these prawns the female carries the eggs in packets underneath the abdomen.

There are several other crustaceans (prawns, crabs, crayfish) which can be kept with fish provided the latter are not adapted for a diet of crustaceans. The swimming-crab *Portunus* and the blue-legged *Callinectes*, on the other hand, will attack fish, and even quite large ones; they spend their time completely buried in the sand. The swimming-crabs (family Portunidae) can be recognized by the broad, leaf-shaped joints of the walking legs, particularly of the last pair, which are held high up and used as paddles in swimming.

## Echinoderms

The most beautiful members of this important animal group, namely the sea-lilies and feather-stars are not suitable for the aquarium. The normal aquarist can, however, keep some of the short-armed sea-stars, which live well on a diet of fish or mollusc flesh. The fragile

Color illustration 5. *Arbacia lixula,* black sea urchin of the Mediterranean. Photo by Dr. K. Knaack.

Color illustration 6. *Paguristes oculatus,* common hermit crab of the Mediterranean. Photo by Dr. K. Knaack.

Color illustration 7. *Asterina gibbosa,* common European sea star. Photo by Holzhammer.

brittle-stars are more difficult to keep and so are the rather unattractive sea-cucumbers (holothurians). The same applies in large measure to the sea-urchins, such as the black *Arbacia lixula* and the blackish-violet to greenish-brown *Paracentrotus lividus*, from the Mediterranean and neighbouring parts of the Atlantic, which are both about 1–2 inches across. These species feed mainly on algae, but will also take scraps of mussel flesh.

There are good reasons for the brevity of this chapter, in spite of the fact that at least 97% of all the known animal species belong among the invertebrates. First, there are relatively few aquarists who are enthusiastic about them and who have gained experience in keeping them. Secondly, they are often very difficult to identify, so that one frequently does not know the name of the animal that is being kept. Museum specialists receive very little material for identification from amateur aquarists, partly because the latter do not know how to preserve the animals that die. Finally, I am sure that many very interesting invertebrates remain unnoticed in sea-water aquaria. For example, one day we quite accidentally found, buried in the sand of a tank, a gephyrean worm belonging to the genus *Golfingia*; it was a good 7 inches long. We quite often discover ragworms (*Nereis*) in the same way.

A number of these marine invertebrates are described and illustrated in such books as:

J. Barrett & C. M. Yonge (1958). *Collins Pocket Guide to the Sea Shore*. London: Collins.

N. B. Eales (1961). *The Littoral Fauna of Great Britain*. Cambridge: University Press.

H. G. Vevers (1954). *The British Seashore*. London: Routledge and Kegan Paul.

# The marine vivarium

As in the case of fresh waters, the edge of the sea also has animals that live an amphibious life. Among the best known are the mudskippers in the genus *Periophthalmus* which are fish related to the gobies. These are so aggressive that many aquarists only attempt to keep a single specimen, and it will usually be rather fussy about its food— definitely a problem fish for the advanced aquarist. The related *Boleophthalmus* and *Pseudapocryptes*, which are less adapted for terrestrial life, are somewhat easier to keep; the latter likes quite shallow water with hiding-places and is particularly fond of *Daphnia*.

Ordinary shore-crabs, *Carcinus maenas*, can be kept if the tank has a small area of dry land. These will feed on an animal diet, particularly earthworms. They should be provided with sufficient hiding-places so that they can escape the attentions of their companions when moulting. These crabs should, of course, be kept relatively cool as they come from temperate seas, whereas the mudskippers are truly tropical.

Fiddler-crabs (*Uca*) are more interesting from the viewpoint of behaviour and they are quite easy to keep. In these, the males have (on one side) a much enlarged and often brightly coloured pincer, which they use for threat and courtship. Fiddler-crabs are widely distributed on tropical coasts and most of the species are only $\frac{3}{4}$–1 inch across (fig. 11). Some of them only become active at dusk,

Fig. 11. A fiddler-crab

Color illustration 8. *Uca,* fiddler crab. Photo by Dr. Herbert R. Axelrod.

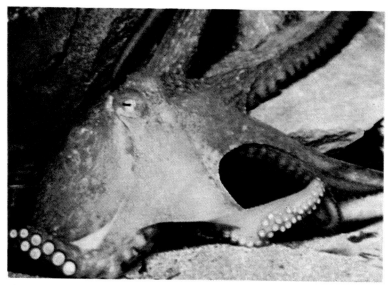

Color illustration 9. *Octopus vulgaris,* common octopus. Photo by Alimenta-Brussels.

Color illustration 10. *Stenopus hispidus,* West Indian banded coral shrimp or barber shrimp. Photo by D. Faulkner.

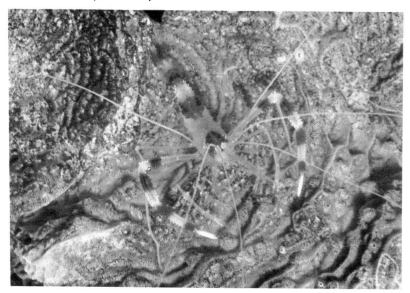

when they are well worth watching. They require a shallow tank with a large surface area (for ten animals it should be 20 × 40 inches, although it can be smaller), and a thick layer of sand in which they will dig their burrows. Against one wall of the tank there should be a small 'swimming pool' filled with sea water, which must be filtered, otherwise it quickly becomes foul. The centre of the tank should have a trough which must be filled every now and again with ordinary mud from the reed zone of a lake or pond. The fiddler-crabs feed on the organic particles in the mud, but they will also take TetraMin and small pieces of fish. They are undemanding and will live for years at a temperature of about 20°C (68°F). The tank must be well covered so that the air inside remains humid, and it should be lit with powerful tungsten lamps (reflector flood lamps as a substitute for sunshine). They have not, however, been bred in captivity.

## Clever fish and stupid fish

Yes, indeed, there are such. The open sea, which is the most monotonous living environment on the globe supports a vast population of small organisms which are distributed throughout it like noodles in a rather thin soup. The temperature and salinity remain constant, there is no lack of fluid, in short, it is an almost utopian habitat. This is the only reason that some jellyfishes are capable of existing at all. Take, for example, the open-sea jellyfish *Rhizostoma*, which J. von Uexküll has described as a swimming pump. Its umbrella of jelly opens and closes at a standard and unchanging rate and this keeps it close to the water surface (movement); at the same time it sucks sea water into the stomach and expels it again after sieving (respiration and food intake). But above all, it keeps this pump working automatically, because at each contraction of the umbrella a tiny structure in the bell-like organs at the umbrella rim stimulates a nerve cushion and thus initiates the next contraction of the umbrella. If this stimulation is prevented by removing the bell-like organs the jellyfish will stop like a motor-car from which the ignition key has been removed, only much quicker. These jellyfishes do not require to be light sensitive, because they are so constructed that gravity always pulls them into the correct position with the umbrella uppermost, and they then automatically swim towards the light. They require no sense of taste, no sense of vibration. As von Uexküll has said, they go through life hearing only the clang of their own marginal bells.

Such poor equipment would not satisfy a higher or more advanced animal, although herring and, even more markedly, certain garfish (which are erroneously held to be poisonous on account of their green bones) are such specialized inhabitants of the open sea that they are quite unable to perceive obstacles. In their natural environment there are no obstacles or traps; if they strike a current in the vicinity of the coast they simply swim directly out to sea. In an aquarium they will swim into the walls, whether transparent or not, and kill themselves. On this account herring can only be kept by the use of a special trick: namely a tank in the form of a ring round which the sea water circulates continuously. The fish then swim against the current, thinking perhaps they are going out to sea, although in practice they are going round in circles.

Partridges behave in a similar stupid way: Professor Konrad Lorenz was able to breed them in the corner of a room partitioned off by a low plank, because as birds of the plains they were unable to make any allowance for a firm vertical obstacle placed across their path. This applied so long as they were on their feet, but as soon as they flew they could immediately avoid such an obstacle. From this we learn that an animal may have individual abilities at its disposal in certain situations, but not necessarily in general.

Partridges and herring behave irrationally in the strongest sense of the word. It is then astonishing how rational their close relatives can be. Whereas partridges (and bustards) or plain-dwelling antelopes are so irrational, American quails and chamois show great powers of reason in mastering or avoiding obstacles. It is common for animals from uniform habitats to appear more stupid to us than those from environments which show great variation. This is because we particularly value the ability to appreciate space which the latter must have if they are to solve the complex spatial problems that confront them in their daily round. Among fishes this ability is particularly marked in those which live permanently in coral clumps or in piles of boulders.

Such fish must have three attributes. First, a sense of curiosity, so

Color illustration 11. *Ophiotrix,* brittle-star. Photo by K. Gillette.

Color illustration 12. *Periophthalmus,* mudskipper. Photo by H. Hansen.

that they can explore their complicated habitat and thus learn the quickest way home when danger threatens. It would be useless merely to flee into the nearest hiding-place, because this would probably be already occupied—perhaps by an enemy. One can watch this exploration in many fish, and particularly well in the blennies. If one of these small fish is placed in a strange tank it will first of all look for a makeshift shelter. After a rather long time and if everything is quiet, it will venture out a little, but immediately withdraw with lightning speed. Gradually it trusts itself to go further afield, slowly advancing, but occasionally turning round quickly and retreating to its starting point along the road it came. If, during the exploration, it comes across a usable dwelling, it approaches the entrance, turns from one side to the other a couple of times as though undecided and tries to get a peep inside, but all the time it is ready to retreat. If the hole is free, it quickly occupies it. Often, however, the original owner may return from a short trip, and, as housing is scarce, a vigorous fight will then ensue. Blennies and other fish which occupy holes are continually exploring their own familiar territory and thus keeping up to date with every change.

This is important because in addition to curiosity they must have the second attribute of memory. This appears so obvious that it is not usually expressed in words. When examined more closely, however, memory is more important than might be expected. There is a small Californian goby, *Bathygobius soporator*, which occurs on the shore in very large numbers. At low tide they regularly remain behind in numerous small residual pools. If you try to catch these gobies, they will jump through the air from one pool to the next or else hop overland straight to the neighbouring pool and by going through a series of pools eventually reach the open water. When they jump from a pool they can never see the target because each pool lies in a dip and is separated from its neighbours by walls. How then do they know which way to go? Two experiments have provided the answer. Some gobies were placed in distant pools which they had never visited. These fish could not be induced to jump out even when vigorously disturbed. In other words, they will only jump out of pools which are known to them. Some other gobies were kept in captivity for fourteen days and were then put back into their own pools. When disturbed they all escaped in the normal way, although some landed on areas of dry beach because the pool they were aiming for had disappeared in the meantime. Further laboratory experiments showed that they learn the very complicated escape routes at flood tide when they wander about over the whole area. They remember these routes for at least forty days, during which period they have had no practice, and they can very quickly re-learn if their surroundings alter.

In addition to curiosity and memory there is a third attribute which allows us to recognize an 'intelligent' fish at first sight: this is the shape of its head. The greatest proficiency in orientation is required by those fish which no longer wander freely above the labyrinth of rocks, corals and sponges, which cannot reach their home 'as the crow flies', but which have become bottom-dwellers without swimbladders and have to find their way home through the maze 'on foot'. Most ordinary fish can simply swim straight ahead to their destination and if in a dense shoal just brake and stop. The heavy bottom-living fishes must measure the leap exactly, that is, they have to estimate the distance to the target, otherwise they may miss the mark and have to start again. Accuracy therefore saves energy. But to hit a target accurately one must be able to see forwards with both eyes, which is scarcely possible for a fish with the normal shape. But bottom-living fishes can do this. Their forehead falls away steeply between the eyes or immediately in front of them, and the eyes, which are often perched high up on the head, are always movable. Also the eyes have a wide field of binocular vision, particularly towards the front, so that the fish can measure distances very accurately. In extreme cases the eyes may also converge towards the rear, that is the fish can fix both eyes on an object behind it without having to turn round. The mudskipper *Periophthalmus* carries its eyes almost free on the head—and it climbs about on land more nimbly than an amphibian.

We humans supposedly had arboreal ancestors who had to judge their target when jumping and climbing even more accurately than a bottom-living fish, because they could not make a fresh start if they made a wrong jump. Perhaps this is why we primarily and quite instinctively measure intelligence from the viewpoint of space. Many readers will have read about the maze experiments, of which evil tongues assert that the experimenter puts a frog, a cockchafer and a mouse in at one end and extols as the most intelligent which ever comes out first at the other end. This story is in any case a

Color illustration 13. *Sphaeramia nematoptera (Apogon nematoptera)*, pyjama cardinal fish.

Color illustration 14. *Scarus croicensis,* striped parrotfish, asleep in its cocoon. Photo by Dr. Walter Starck III.

Color illustration 15. *Sparisoma chrysopterum,* redtail parrotfish, male. This parrotfish sleeps without cocoon. Photo by Dr. J. E. Randall.

caricature of the common mistake of not taking into account the different types of animal specializations when making comparisons, for not all of these specializations are concerned with the appreciation of space. But spatial relations are particularly important to us so it is no wonder that we regard as especially intelligent any fish that emerges from a hiding-place, looks around actively, focuses several times on a coral branch and then rushes straight at it. But we must appreciate that it is only fish with the head shape and eye position described above that can actually do this.

## Fish wearing nighties

I should begin by explaining that this has nothing to do with the so-called Pyjama Cardinal Fish (*Apogon nematopterus*), in which the striped colour pattern is an integral part of the fish's skin. There are, however, fish which make themselves nightgowns, indeed a new one every evening. It is possible that in your tank you have already seen a delicate, milky-white, jelly-like tube about the thickness of a pencil; these are usually long and they are eventually held buoyant at the surface by small bubbles of gas before they decay. Such sheaths are regularly found in tanks occupied by certain wrasse, for example the cleaner-wrasse *Labroides* and some species of *Thalassoma*. They are sheaths of mucus in which the fish spend the night on (or perhaps in) the bottom. We do not know how they are produced.

Parrotfish of the genera *Scarus* and *Pseudoscarus* also go to rest in similar nightgowns. At night they lie down on the bottom and go to sleep leaning up against coral branches, snail shells or similar objects. Before actually going to sleep they prepare the nightgown in about thirty to sixty minutes. It begins as a fold of mucus at the mouth and spreads over the whole fish. A small hole is left in front of the mouth and behind the anal fin for the entry and exit of the water used in respiration. This mucus covering consists of several layers and it does not lie in direct contact with the body; in many places there is an intermediate space of several centimetres. A *Scarus punctulatus* 7 inches long builds itself a nightie that is 9 inches long, 5 inches wide and $3\frac{1}{2}$ inches tall. Again, in these fish we still do not know exactly how these structures are produced, because they are only made during the hours of darkness. As soon as the lights are turned on the fish will stop making the sheath and move out of it either forwards, backwards or sideways. The sheath usually then collapses and lies on the bottom because it is somewhat sticky. These sheaths of mucus probably serve as a protection against predators, such as moray-eels which at night-time hunt by scent for fish that sleep on the bottom; this is another point that should be investigated. Anyone interested in the method of production of nightgowns should not bother with *Sparisoma*, because the species in this genus sleep naked.

I should also mention that the nightgowns of the wrasse and parrotfish probably provide a further piece of evidence for the view that these two groups are closely related. The other obvious character which they have in common is the peculiar method of swimming, for they both use only the breast fins.

## The coralfish community tank

The normal marine aquarium accommodates different species living alongside each other. There are several reasons for this. First, it is more attractive, and in many cases only a single specimen of a species can be kept, because they fight with members of their own species. And secondly, there is a special fascination in many of the interrelations between different species (see page 97 *et seq.*).

Sea-horses and similar delicate fish should be kept without other species. The same can be done with *Dascyllus*, *Amphiprion*, gobies and blennies in order to study their behaviour in more detail. Care must be taken when mixing the species as they do not always agree with each other. It is obvious that predators with large mouths should only be kept with correspondingly robust species. They can be fed on pieces of fish and on the heart or liver of warm-blooded animals.

Pomacentrids should not be kept with butterflyfish or other shy forms, because they are inquisitive and always first at the food. The butterflyfish will not get sufficient food until the pomacentrids have developed fatty degeneration of the liver.

Members of the family Plectognathidae (boxfish, pufferfish,

Color illustration 16. *Gomphosus varius,* a wrasse with long snout. Photo by Yasuda and Hiyama.

Color illustration 17. *Forcipiger flavissimus,* a chaetodont with long snout and small mouth. Photo by Dr. Herbert R. Axelrod.

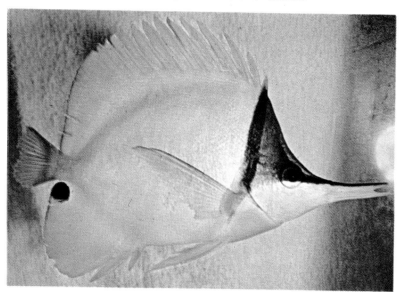

Color illustration 18. *Scarus ghobban.* Parrotfish have teeth fused into structure resembling a beak. Photo by Yasuda and Hiyama.

Color illustration 19. *Gymnothorax* sp. Moray eels are predatory fishes with large mouth and sharp teeth. Photo by D. Faulkner.

triggerfish) tend to be misused as mincing machines by the other inhabitants of the tank. For whereas most fish chew their prey with the back teeth, the Plectognathidae seize it with their front cutting teeth and will chew along each worm several times. Inquisitive neighbours often wait until the worm appears for the second time and then snap it off.

A community tank should be fed as sparingly as a tank with only a single species, and this means only as much as will be consumed in five minutes (live food excepted). Once a tank has been established with a full complement of fish, new specimens should only be added in exceptional cases, because they will often be unable to stand up against the original inhabitants. Most coralfish need to have an exact knowledge of their environment with all its hiding-places if they are to settle down properly. This means that frequent rebuilding of a tank is out of the question, but naturally it sometimes makes the treatment of sick fish in quarantine tanks rather difficult.

There is no reason why fish from different oceans should not be kept together, even if the salinity of the home water is somewhat different. For example, normal sea water has a salinity of $35^0/_{00}$ whereas that of the Red Sea has $40^0/_{00}$; for comparison, the Dead Sea, which supports no life, has a salinity of $192^0/_{00}$.

Fast-moving, hungry sharks cruise above the reefs in large numbers, picking off the stragglers from the fleeing shoals of reef fish, and so quick, indiscreet movements in front of the aquarium tank can easily cause panic among the inhabitants.

It is not usually possible to distinguish the sexes of most coralfish (their normal bright colours are not concerned with courtship and display); this applies to butterflyfish (Chaetodontidae), damselfish (Pomacentridae), marine anglefish (Pomacanthidae) and almost all the other perch-like fish, such as surgeonfish, the Plectognathidae and so on. As a rule, however, the genital papilla is conical and pointed in the male, but broad and round in the female. On the other hand, the sexes of wrasse and parrotfish are so different that they were at one time regarded as separate species.

# The food of coralfish

On a coral-reef an unbelievable number of species, many of which are closely related, are to be found living close together. This is due not so much to the absence of competitors but rather to the fact that many species are specialized for feeding on very different diets. Nevertheless they will all feed on 'non-specific' food if the opportunity arises, so the feeding of marine fish is not really so difficult. Among the more fastidious are the long-snouted forms which are found in a number of different families (*Zanclus*, a distant relative of the surgeonfish, *Chelmon* and *Forcipiger* among the Chaetodontidae, *Gomphosus* among the wrasse). These prefer to fish tiny animals out of crevices, and they often take a long time learning to eat food that floats free in the water.

Almost all coralfish will eat freshly chopped flesh of freshwater fish, bivalve molluscs and crabs. Earthworms are much liked. Surgeonfish and butterflyfish will browse on algae and some pufferfish, triggerfish and porcupinefish are passionately fond of pond snails—the related Sunfish (*Mola*) eats jellyfish! The synopsis of most commonly kept coralfish gives the kinds of food that are preferred. Here I would give a summary of what can be fed to any of them and leave the reader to find what is most suitable for his own fish—for sometimes they develop individual tastes. However, coralfish should always be fed with as much variety as possible, and if possible several times a day. Indeed four or five times a day would be quite safe.

Foods: live-bearing toothcarps acclimatized to sea water; minced fish, mussel and crab flesh; grated horse heart, lean beef, fish roe, fresh ant pupae (erroneously known as ants' eggs), mealworms; *Artemia*, *Daphnia*, freshwater plankton and insect larvae, shrimps, *Tubifex*, midge larvae; earthworms, whiteworms; wingless fruitflies (*Drosophila*); Biomin, TetraMin, finely ground oatflakes; green algae from fresh waters, the liverwort *Riccia*, Canadian Waterweed, green lettuce.

Even specialized feeders on algae (surgeonfish and the blenny *Ecsenius*) can be fed almost exclusively on fish flesh. In the case of chopped or minced foods the size of the pieces will depend on the size of the fish's mouth. Predators like large chunks. When feeding with pond mussels only the foot, mantle and liver should be used

Color illustration 20. *Pterois antennata,* spotfin lionfish. Photo by Dr. D. Terver.

Color illustration 21. *Ecsenius bicolor,* bicolor blenny. Photo by Dr. J. E. Randall.

Color illustration 22. *Scatophagus argus,* spotted scat. Photo by Dr. H. R. Axelrod.

and these should be rinsed in running water in a net after mincing; this will remove mucus and the tank water will remain clearer.

Much of the food will quite rightly be kept in a refrigerator and it must of course be brought up to the temperature of the tank water before use. Most coralfish eat a lot, but spread over the whole day. They should therefore be fed accordingly, because live food from fresh water does not live long in sea water, even if previously kept at the same temperature. *Tubifex* dies very rapidly, *Daphnia pulex* lives for about ten minutes, mayfly larvae and *Cyclops* in about two hours, while *Corethra* and gnat larvae may survive for up to twenty-four hours.

Fish-eaters such as *Pterois*, *Scorpaena*, anglerfish, should be fed once or twice a week. A few drops of Protovita (La Roche), β-carotene and chlorophyll can easily be added to flesh that has been minced or chopped; this sometimes has a marked stimulating effect on the appetite of fish that feed reluctantly.

Do not use the so-called colour foods. A healthy, properly kept fish will show its colours without this. If for some reason it does not do so, you will only produce a caricature of it with 'colour food', as many American colour advertisements show.

## Some fish for the marine aquarium

There are so many sea-water fish suitable for the aquarium that it has been extremely difficult to make a selection. Eventually I decided to base my selection on two criteria: (1) to include, so far as possible, typical representatives of the most common groups, so that the layman would get to know the appearance of a curlyfin or a goby without necessarily being able to determine the exact species, and (2) to give the species characteristics of those coralfish which are already well known but which surprisingly enough are often confused. This happens for example with the various marine angelfish, and especially with their juvenile stages. The black-and-white drawings have been most carefully executed by Herr Kacher. In particular these show the position of the fins which may vary considerably even between related species. More detailed descriptions are given in the text. The drawings also show the most important species of Chaetodontidae and Pomacentridae which can be identified by their coloration and pattern, but not those species which can only be determined by investigating the teeth or gill arches. Such differences between species have in most cases also been omitted from the text.

*How to use the plates:* If you know the generic name of a fish you should look for it in the index, where you will find the plate number and the text page (if it is one that is dealt with in this book). If you only know the approximate appearance of the fish, you should look through the plates and find from the captions the text page on which it is described. If you still do not know which fish you would regard as the most attractive, you should start with the text.

The plates show all the fish in their daytime pattern; at night or when scared they may appear quite different. Many fish can be identified most easily if they can be seen alongside their closest relatives. Here it is hoped that the plates will help. In a dealer's shop you would usually only see one species without having a chance to compare it with another live fish. For this reason the most closely similar fish are here shown alongside each other. It may, of course, happen that you cannot identify a fish even after careful scrutiny of the plates; this will happen if fish that are not described here come on to the market. The text is therefore concerned only with distinguishing between species that have already been imported. So any new imports will provide new opportunities for confusion. But one can never tell which it will be, and several volumes would be needed if I were to describe all the fish that are suitable for our purpose.

The size given is always the maximum. In the plates the young fish are drawn only slightly smaller, so as to show more details. When they become adult their coloration may change, and this is often very variable even within a single species. In the description the first colour mentioned is that of the general body coloration. Important behavioural characteristics are given insofar as they are known (from this you will soon learn how little is known).

THERAPONIDAE

Several species in the Indo-Pacific. Coastal fish which also go into brackish and fresh water. They are easier to acclimatize (slowly) to fresh water than, for example, *Scatophagus*. Easy to keep.

Color illustration 23. *Lutjanus sebae,* emperor snapper. Photo by K. Probst.

Color illustration 24. *Anisotremus virginicus,* porkfish. Photo by Dr. J. E. Randall.

Color illustration 25. *Haemulon flavolineatum,* French grunt. Photo by C. Limbaugh.

*Description: Therapon jarbua* (Forskål), Jarbua (plate I, 1) 11 inches. Silvery-white to yellowish, the stripes and the tips of the dorsal and caudal fins brown to black. Young fish up to 3 inches long defend sandpits dug by themselves; later on they live in shoals. Active swimmers. In this species there are fourteen scale rows above the lateral line, whereas the very similar *T. theraps* Cuvier has only eight.

LUTJANIDAE, Snappers
Widely distributed in tropical seas, usually living near the coast singly or in groups; very varied food habits. Fast-growing predators with large mouths and sharp canine teeth in the jaws. Body form variable, from the Emperor Snapper (see below) through a *haemulon* shape to those such as *L. lineolatus* which are similar to the European Pope or Ruffe (*Acerina*). Easy to keep.

*Descriptions: Lutjanus decussatus* (Cuvier), Cross-banded Snapper (plate I, 2). Indo-Pacific, 11 inches. Pale whitish, with dark red-brown stripes.

*L. kasmira* (Forskål). Pacific, 15 inches. Body and fins yellow to olive, on each side four to five longitudinal blue stripes edged with brown; dark spots on the hind third of body. Aggressive towards members of its own species.

*L. sebae* (Cuvier), Emperor Snapper (plate I, 3). Indo-Australian region, over 3 feet. Whitish, with brick-red to dark red bands.

HAEMULIDAE, Grunts
Widely distributed around the West Indies and off the Atlantic coast of America; closely related to the snappers. By grinding the pharyngeal teeth they produce sounds which are amplified by the swim-bladder acting as a resonator. Easy to keep.

Fig. 12

*Descriptions: Anisotremus virginicus* (Linnaeus), Porkfish (plate I, 4). West Indies to Florida, 11 inches. Hind part of body with longitudinal blue stripes, the bands on the head black. Feeds on small animals. The young act as cleaners.

*Haemulon* species (fig. 12): attractive medium-sized predators, usually about 11 inches long; small species in shoals (*H. flavolineatum*), large species solitary and guarding a territory. Show characteristic aggressive behaviour to neighbours at the boundary between territories; they stay in position with open mouths (brightly coloured inside) pressed against each other (fig. 12). Better known species: *H. flavolineatum* (Desmarest) French Grunt; *H. plumieri* (Lacépède) White Grunt; and *H. sciurus* (Shaw) Blue-striped Grunt.

SERRANIDAE, Groupers
About 400 species strongly represented in the tropics, less so in temperate regions. Predators with large mouths and powerful teeth. Lie hidden and motionless waiting for prey. Habitat and size very variable, 1½ inches to 6 feet. In general, not peaceful. Require crevices and caves to live in. Easy to keep. Well-known genera: *Cephalopholis*, *Epinephelus* (with several species, difficult to distinguish, on rocky and coral coasts in all warm seas), *Roccus*, *Morone*, *Mycteroperca* and the following:

*Descriptions: Serranus scriba* (Linnaeus), Banded Sea-perch (plate I, 5). Tropical East Atlantic, Mediterranean, 11 inches. Live solitarily in cliff holes or rubble islets, defending a territory. Yellow to reddish with five to nine dark red-brown transverse bands, the sides of the head with silvery-blue 'scribbles', the fins yellowish with red spots. When excited dark brown to black coloration spreads backwards from the head. Feed on molluscs, crustaceans, small fish.

*Serranellus subligarius* (Cope), Belted Sandfish. Coasts of Southeastern United States, 6 inches. Olive, reddish above, belly silvery-white, with a cream-coloured marking in front which reaches to the sides of the body, a black ring round the caudal peduncle, and a black spot at the beginning of the dorsal fin. Feed on small animals. See p. 96 for the remarkable reproduction.

*Grammistes sexlineatus* (Thunberg), Six-lined Grouper (plate I, 6). The only species in the genus. Indo-Pacific coasts, 9 inches. Almost always in open water. Brown to black, 3–9 longitudinal yellow stripes, the number increasing with age. Quite small specimens (½ inch) have

Color illustration 26. *Pseudochromis paccagnellae,* Photo by Dr. Herbert R. Axelrod.

Color illustration 27. *Gramma loreto (Gramma hemichrysos),* royal gramma. Photo by Dr. K. Knaack.

Color illustration 28. *Myripristis murdjan,* bigeye squirrelfish. Photo by Dr. Herbert R. Axelrod.

Color illustration 29. *Equetus lanceolatus,* jackknife fish. Photo by K. Probst.

two rows of white spots in place of the stripes. Eats whole shore crabs, earthworms, etc.

*Chromileptis altivelis*, Cuvier and Valenciennes. Indian Ocean, 20 inches. Strikingly small, attractive head, large fins. Silvery-grey with large round black spots all over the body and fins, including the large, elegant, fan-like pectorals.

*Anthias squamipinnis* Peters (plate VI, 1). Central tropical Pacific, 4 inches. Golden-red, with two violet-blue stripes between the eyes and the pectorals. Usually sits out in front of a crevice. Live food, somewhat fastidious. Related species in all warm seas, all very pretty and brightly coloured.

PSEUDOCHROMIDAE
Most closely related to the Serranidae. Small, active, little-known reef-fishes. Body longish and brightly coloured. Anal and dorsal fins each with only three spines. Lurk under overhangs or in crevices, waiting for prey which they seize in a quick rush.

*Description: Gramma hemichrysos* (Mowbray) (plate IX, 6). Caribbean Sea, 2¼ inches. (Recently offered for sale as *G. loreto*.) Violet-purple in front, bright yellow behind. Eye stripe and dorsal fin spot black. Coral-reefs, at depths greater than 12 feet. They live solitarily in caves in high coral blocks and when swimming turn the belly towards a firm structure, so that at the ceiling of a cave they will swim upside down. Sometimes clean other fish.

APOGONIDAE, Cardinal Fishes
Tropical and subtropical seas. Mostly small (3–5 inches) active species, living alone or in small groups. Particularly numerous on reefs and in shallow water in the Indo-Pacific. Two separated dorsal fins, only two anal fin spines, large eyes, brightly coloured (usually red). Will eat all kinds of small animals of a suitable size. Males often smaller but with larger heads than the females. Males brood eggs in the mouth, the eggs hanging together with long filaments. Display with internal fertilization a few days before spawning.

Well-known genera: *Apogon, Cheilodipterus, Siphamia.*

*Descriptions: Apogon nematopterus* (Bleeker), Pyjama Cardinal Fish (plate I, 7). Celebes, New Guinea, 3 inches. Greenish to yellowish brown, ventral stripes dark brown, first dorsal fin and the spots on the hind end reddish-brown.

*Siphamia* species: Indo-Pacific. Recognized by the silvery light glands, which extend in a canal from the tongue along both sides of the belly to the anal fin.

SPARIDAE, Sea-bream
In all seas, except the very cold. Coastal fish, preferring shallow water, some in the surf zone. Also represented in the Mediterranean *Sargus, Diplodus, Dentex, Boops*). Active fish, some species becoming quite large. Usually inconspicuously coloured. Many live in groups, but in the aquarium they are rather intolerant of each other. Predatory, omnivorous or eating algae. Easy to keep, but difficult to mix with other fish, except in very large tanks.

HOLOCENTRIDAE, Soldierfishes or Squirrelfishes
On reefs and in shallow water in all tropical seas. Active at night, hidden during the day in crevices and caves. Large, somewhat protruding eyes, rough scales, a long spine at the beginning of the anal fin. Brightly coloured, mainly red, frequently with longitudinal, silvery stripes on the flanks. Predators feeding in nature on crustaceans, worms, small fish, snails.

*Descriptions: Holocentrum* species: a long, thorny spine at base of operculum. Usually solitary, defending a territory. Produce sounds.

*Myripristis* species: very similar to the foregoing, but without the long opercular spine. Usually living in groups or shoals.

*Myripristis murdjan* Forskål (plate I, 8). Tropical Indo-Pacific, 12 inches. Red, fins marked with black and with white tips. Very large eyes with black bands. Predatory.

SCIAENIDAE, Drums
Tropical and subtropical seas, usually near to the coast. Two dorsal fins only slightly connected at the base. Usually with a characteristically rounded mouth. Produce sounds that can be heard at a distance, by the contraction of muscles which make the swimbladder vibrate. When in groups they make an astonishing underwater noise. Some are up to 3 feet long. In aquaria it is almost always the species of *Eques* that are kept.

*Descriptions: Eques* species (sometimes known as *Equetus*). Tropical America. Specialized representatives of the family with much elongated, dark dorsal fin which becomes relatively shorter with in-

Color illustration 30. *Paracirrhites forsteri,* freckled hawkfish. Photo by Yasuda and Hiyama.

Color illustration 31. *Cirrhitichthys aprinus,* spotted hawkfish. Photo by K. Paysan.

Color illustration 32. *Lutjanus kasmira*, blue-striped snapper. Photo by K. Paysan.

Color illustration 33. *Spilotichthys pictus,* sweetlips. Photo by G. Marcuse.

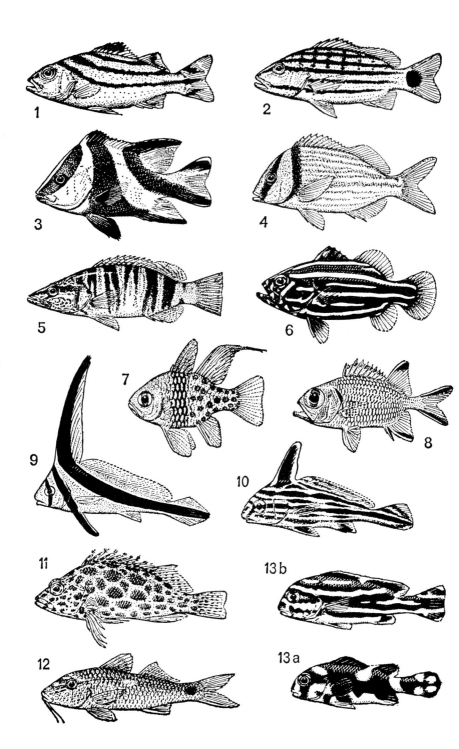

creasing age. In shallow water, often on reefs. Require a large tank with plenty of open sand; do well in captivity. Aggressive towards each other.

*E. lanceolatus* (Linnaeus), Jack-knife Fish (plate I, 9). 9 inches. White with black bands. Feed on crustaceans.

*E. acuminatus* (Bloch & Schneider), Cubbyu (plate I, 10). 9½ inches. Whitish to brownish-grey, with seven dark brown longitudinal stripes, lying close together, but often partially broken up.

*E. pulcher* (Steindachner). 8 inches. Only three brown longitudinal stripes, which run from the eyes to the caudal fin.

MULLIDAE, Red Mullets
On sandy and muddy bottoms in shallow water in the warmer seas. Small but active bottom fishes living in groups. Small mouth, the tip of the lower jaw with two long, very mobile barbels which search in the sand for molluscs, crustaceans and worms. Two widely separated dorsal fins and a forked caudal fin. Eyes at the upper edge of the head. Bright, quickly changing colours. The genus *Mullus* in the Mediterranean and Western English Channel; other genera *Upeneus*, *Parupeneus*. Easy to keep but difficult to identify; many doubtful species are only distinguished on colour characters.

*Description: Pseudupeneus indicus* (Shaw) (plate I, 12). Indo-Pacific, 15 inches. Delicate pink to spotted with deep purple, head and front part of back iridescent gold; there may also be blue and green metallic colours. Belly and fins reddish, a black spot on the caudal peduncle. Coloration alters with the mood.

CIRRHITIDAE, Curlyfins
In shallow water on rocky and coral coasts of the tropical Indo-Pacific. Small, solitary, brightly coloured predators which lurk motionless among corals waiting for crustaceans and small fish. They are heavier than water and rest motionless on the bottom in among

Plate I. 1. *Therapon jarbua* (p. 48), 2. *Lutianus decussatus* (p. 48), 3. *L. sebae* (p. 48), 4. *Anisotremus virginicus* (p. 49), 5. *Serranus scriba* (p. 49), 6. *Grammistes sexlineatus* (p. 49), 7. *Apogon nematopterus* (p. 50), 8. *Myripristis murdjan* (p. 51), 9. *Eques lanceolatus* (p. 53), 10. *E. acuminatus* (p. 53), 11. *Cirrhitichthys aprinus* (p. 54), 12. *Pseudupeneus indicus* (p. 53), 13. *Plectorhynchus orientalis;* (*a*) juvenile, (*b*) adult (p. 54)

Color illustration 34. *Parachaetodon ocellatus,* ocellate butterflyfish. Photo by Dr. Herbert R. Axelrod.

Color illustration 35. *Chaetodon fremblii,* blue-striped butterflyfish. Photo by Dr. Herbert R. Axelrod.

Color illustration 36. *Gaterin chaetodonoides (Plectorhynchus chaetodonoides),* clown sweetlips. Photo by Dr. Herbert R. Axelrod.

coral branches and under overhangs, looking around actively. The lower rays of the pectoral fins are thickened and free from the fin membrane and serve as supports. The tips of the dorsal fin spines bear brush-like tufts of short filaments, which wave about in the stream of water leaving the gills. Do well in captivity.

*Description: Cirrhitichthys aprinus* (Cuvier) (plate I, 11). $3\frac{1}{2}$ inches. Yellowish to red-brown, with two to three longitudinal rows of large dark brown spots, with small spots in between, on the body and on the dorsal and caudal fins. Very aggressive towards each other, but form into pairs that keep together.

*Cirrhitichthys aureus* (Schlegel). $3\frac{1}{2}$ inches. Golden-brown to reddish, with traces of darker transverse bands on the flanks. First ray of the soft dorsal fin elongated to form a filament.

*Paracirrhites forsteri* (Bloch). 17 inches. Head blue-grey with black spots, those on the opercula edged with red. Back dark violet-brown to black. Base of the dorsal fin and middle of the flanks yellow, belly reddish.

PLECTORHYNCHIDAE, Sweetlips
Mostly closely related to the *Haemulidae*. Indo-Australian. Omnivorous. In groups to shoals in warm, shallow waters. Very striking coloration, but the young are often so different from the adults that even today growth stages are described as separate species. Genera: *Spilotichthys, Gaterin, Diagramma, Plectorhynchus*; some species are referred, now to one now to another genus. All require free swimming space and live food. The young, in particular, swim with a paddling movement of the pectoral fins and rock to and fro like *Amphiprion*. The species of *Plectorhynchus* only occur in the central Indo-Pacific.

*Descriptions: Plectorhynchus orientalis* (Bloch) (plate I, 13). 15 inches. The young are chocolate-brown with pale cream spots edged with yellow. Adults with similarly coloured longitudinal stripes.

*P. chaetodonoides* Lacépède. Indo-Malaysian, 16 inches. Young specimens brown with white spots, which—unlike the previous

Plate II. 1. *Heniochus acuminatus* (p. 56), 2. *Chelmon rostratus* (p. 56), 3. *Forcipiger longirostris* (p. 56), 4. *Zanclus cornutus* (p. 60), 5. *Chaetodon lunula;* (*a*) juvenile, (*b*) adult (p. 58), 6. *C. falcula* (p. 58), 7. *C. collare* (p. 58), 8. *C. ephippium* (p. 58), 9. *C. citrinellus* (p. 58), 10. *C. chrysurus* (p. 58), 11. *Chaetodontoplus mesoleucus* (p. 62)

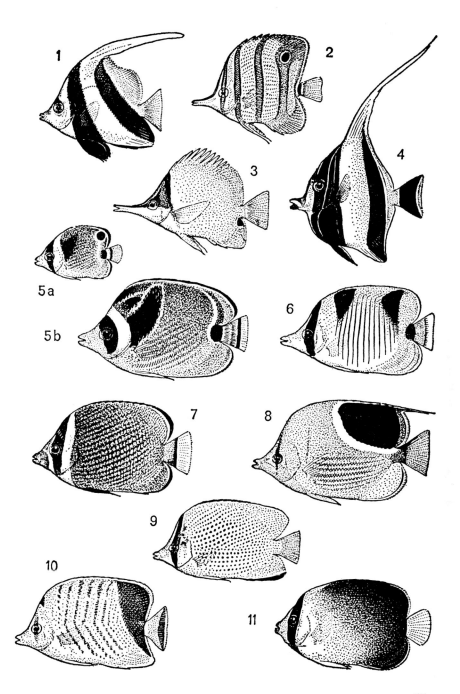

Color illustration 37. *Chaetodon citrinellus*, speckled butterflyfish. Photo by D. Faulkner.

Color illustration 38. *Chelmon rostratus*, Indo-Pacific longsnout butterflyfish. Photo by Roger Steene.

Color illustration 39. *Heniochus acuminatus,* pennant coralfish. Photo by K. Paysan.

species—have dark brown edges. Caudal fin pale with two circular brown spots. Adults speckled.

*P. pictus* Thunberg. 17 inches. Young (3 inches) silvery white, with black longitudinal stripes (like those of adult *P. orientalis*) edged with yellow. With increasing age these stripes break up into small, grey-brown spots; background colour silvery-grey.

CHAETODONTIDAE, Butterflyfishes
Tropical seas. Small to medium-sized, very brightly coloured fish with tall, compressed bodies. Typical reef-dwellers with small mouth, feeding on tiny organisms. Caudal fin never forked. Swim around all day, but require hiding-places. Some take up a territory and are then aggressive to members of the same species. At least some of them form into pairs like bottom-brooding cichlids; whether they jointly protect the brood is unknown. Almost all of them search for small animals among the corals and also browse on algae; many like to tear off coral polyps, small sea-anemones (*Aiptasia*) and tube-worms.

*Descriptions: Heniochus* species. Indo-Pacific. Fourth dorsal fin spine longer than the others. Live in large groups. Conspicuous black and white bands. Dorsal, caudal and pectoral fins usually yellow.

*Heniochus acuminatus* (Linnaeus), Pennant Coralfish (plate II, 1). 9 inches. Very long fourth dorsal fin spine with white fin membrane. The best known member of the genus.

*H. varius* (Cuvier). Pennant much shorter than in the preceding species, and the back is grey instead of black.

*Chelmon rostratus* (Linnaeus) (plate II, 2). Malayan Archipelago, Philippines, 6 inches. Nine dorsal fin spines, longest in front of the fifth. Dorsal fin with scales up to $\frac{2}{3}$ of its height. Pale silvery to yellowish, the bands orange to red, the dorsal fin with a black eye-spot. Often aggressive. Search with pincer-like mouth for small crustaceans and worms in crevices. Difficult to keep. Will take small living *Mysis* and young earthworms.

---

Plate III. 1. *Parachaetodon ocellatus* (p. 58), 2. *Chaetodon octofasciatus* (p. 59), 3. *C. fremblii* (p. 59), 4. *C. meyeri* (p. 59), 5. *C. striatus* (p. 59), 6. *C. trifasciatus* (p. 59), 7. *C. vagabundus* (p. 59), 8. *C. pictus* (p. 59), 9. *C. auriga* (p. 59), 10. *C. ocellatus* (p. 59), 11. *C. capistratus* (p. 59), 12. *C. unimaculatus* (p. 60)

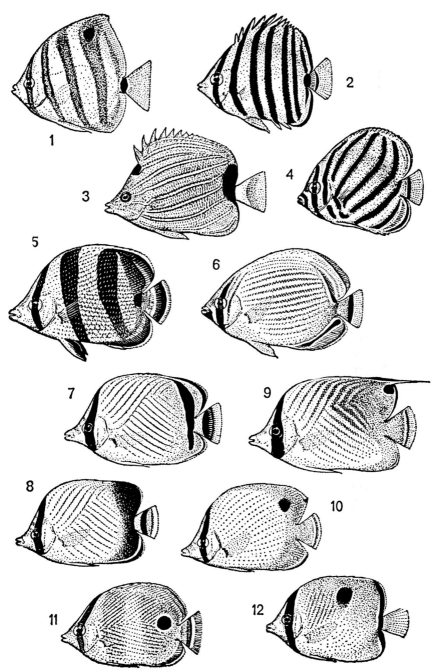

57

Color illustration 40. *Chaetodon capistratus,* foureye butterflyfish. Photo by Dr. Herbert R. Axelrod.

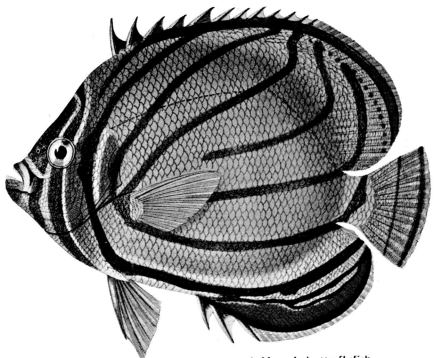

Color illustration 41. *Chaetodon meyeri,* Meyer's butterflyfish.

Color illustration 42. *Chaetodon lunula,* raccoon butterflyfish. Photo by Dr. Herbert R. Axelrod.

*Forcipiger longirostris* (Broussonet) (plate II, 3). Indo-Pacific, 8 inches. Dorsal fin with twelve to thirteen spines, of which the fifth is the longest, and with scales only at the base. Golden-yellow, head brown above, whitish below. Anal fin with an unbordered black spot. Difficult to keep. The very similar *F. cyrano* Randall and *F. inornatus* Randall have even longer snouts.

*Chaetodon* species; very many species, distinguished principally by the attractive colour patterns, although this is often difficult in the case of closely related forms. Live singly or in pairs in crevices on living coral-reefs, fight strangers of their own species, during which the dorsal fin is erected. For the sake of simplicity several are here included as members of the genus *Chaetodon*, which some authors have placed in other genera (e.g. *Anisochaetodon, Linophora*). Unless otherwise stated the species is Indo-Pacific.

*C. lunula* (Lacépède) (plate II, 5). 7 inches. Greenish-yellow, a white forehead stripe behind the eyes. The spots on the shoulder and caudal peduncle and the band through the eye are black. Juveniles (*a*) with black eyespot on the dorsal fin, adults (*b*) with diagonal rows of reddish-golden spots on the flanks.

*C. falcula* Bloch (plate II, 6). 7 inches. White with the dorsal, caudal and anal fins yellow. The stripes are black. (General coloration similar to that of *C. auriga*, see plate III, 9.)

*C. collare* Bloch (plate II, 7). 5 inches. Basically a medley of browns. Head band black bordered with white. Dorsal and anal fins edged with red posteriorly. One of the most imported species.

*C. ephippium* Cuvier (plate II, 8). 7 inches. Blue-grey, the underside of the head yellow, a very conspicuous black spot on the back, bordered at the front with white, at the rear with red. Caudal peduncle white above, golden-red below. The vertical eye-stripe is broad in juveniles, but only a hint of it remains in the adults.

*C. citrinellus* Cuvier (plate II, 9). $3\frac{1}{2}$ inches. Yellowish-white, with blue-black to blackish-brown flank spots (smaller than the pupil) in about eighteen diagonal rows. Very similar to *C. guttatissimus* Bennett (India, Red Sea, east coast of Africa, $4\frac{1}{2}$ inches) in which the spots are irregularly arranged. These two species are often confused.

*C. chrysurus* (Desjardins) (plate II, 10). $5\frac{1}{2}$ inches. White to yellowish, the flank spots blue-grey to black. Caudal, anal and dorsal fins sometimes rust-red at the rear. Rare.

*Parachaetodon ocellatus* (Cuvier) (plate III, 1). $5\frac{1}{2}$ inches. Yellowish-white, the fins yellow, the bands grey-brown, the caudal and dorsal fins with black eyespots. Juveniles silvery-white with the eyespots less conspicuous.

*Chaetodon octofasciatus* Bloch (plate III, 2). 4 inches. Silvery, the bands blackish-brown, the snout, ventral fins and first anal spines yellowish.

*C. fremblii* Bennett (plate III, 3). Pacific, 4 inches. Yellow, the spots on the nape and tail black, caudal peduncle white, body stripes blue. Without black eye-stripes!

*C. meyeri* Bloch & Schneider (plate III, 4). 9 inches. Blue, the underside of the body and the dorsal, caudal and anal fins orange. Bands black. Unmistakable.

*C. striatus* Linnaeus (plate III, 5). Pacific, $5\frac{1}{2}$ inches. White with black stripes. Juveniles with a black eyespot on the soft dorsal fin, adults with a black spot at the root of the tail.

*C. trifasciatus* Mungo Park (plate III, 6). 4 inches. Yellowish, the soft dorsal fin yellow to orange, anal fin red to orange with two longitudinal black bands. Caudal peduncle orange, the caudal fin-rays blue. The bands on the head and tail are black, those on the body somewhat paler. A rare and beautiful species.

*C. vagabundus* Linnaeus (plate III, 7). 8 inches. White, the dorsal, caudal and anal fins yellow, the bands black.

*C. pictus* Forskål (plate III, 8). Only off Ceylon, $3\frac{1}{2}$ inches. Like the preceding species, to which it is closely related, but the dorsal fin is uniformly dark with no yellow.

*C. auriga* Forskål (plate III, 9). 7 inches. One of the best known species. White, with the dorsal, caudal and anal fins yellow, the eye-stripes and dorsal eyespots black. In adults the dorsal fin carries a long yellow filament above the dorsal eyespot. During the day the body stripes should be quite pale; the darker they become the sicker the fish. This species is particularly catholic as regards diet and it wanders quite a distance from the living reef on to stretches of sand and coral rubble.

*C. ocellatus* Bloch (plate III, 10). West Indies, $5\frac{1}{2}$ inches. Particularly common in the Central American region. Yellowish, the eyespots and bands black, a black band on the dorsal fin disappears with age.

*C. capistratus* Linnaeus (plate III, 11). West Indies, $5\frac{1}{2}$ inches. White with the tip of the snout, the throat, belly and fins yellowish.

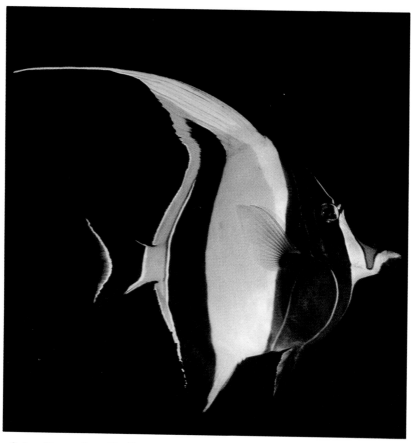

Color illustration 43. *Zanclus canescens (Zanclus cornutus)*, Moorish idol. Photo by Dr. J. E. Randall

Color illustration 44. *Pomacanthus annularis,* blue-ringed angelfish. Photo by Yasuda and Hiyama.

The large black eyespots at the rear of the body are edged with white.
*C. unimaculatus* Bloch (plate III, 12). 4½ inches. Whitish-yellow, the dorsal and anal fins yellow, the caudal fin pale yellow. Bands and eyespots black, flank stripes grey.

ZANCLIDAE
Tropical Indo-Pacific. Unmistakable, although sometimes confused with *Heniochus*. Tall compressed body. Third dorsal fin-ray very long. Protruding snout, small mouth. Swim with strokes of the pectoral fins which are held stiff. From the viewpoint of relationships they stand intermediate between the Chaetodontidae and the Acanthuridae (see p. 56). Only one genus.

*Description: Zanclus cornutus* (Linnaeus), Moorish Idol (plate II, 4). 9 inches. White to yellowish, the dorsal, caudal and anal fins yellow at the rear. The bands are black edged with blue. The 'saddle' spot on the snout is brown. Adults have a small horn in front of each eye. Difficult to keep; like a well-lit, sunny tank. They acclimatize themselves only slowly to changes in diet.

*Z. canescens* (Linnaeus) which has a very protruding breast region is probably the juvenile form of *Z. cornutus*.

POMACANTHIDAE, Marine Angelfishes
Tropical seas, particularly the Indo-Pacific. Closely related to the Chaetodontidae. Many are extremely beautiful. A long spine at base of operculum. Medium-sized reef-fish which tend to occupy a territory. Juvenile and adults very differently coloured, but the young of related species are similar to the point of confusion. Coloration changes at a length of about 3 inches, but often much later in aquaria. Marine Angelfish are solitary, quarrelsome fish which form into pairs. It is difficult to keep several specimens of the same species together, but easy to have just one of several different species, provided they have reached the stage where their colour patterns are different. They take rather small food which they pick up in mid-

---

Plate IV. 1. *Pomacanthodes annularis;* (*a*) juvenile, (*b*) adult (p. 62), 2. *P. imperator;* (*a*) juvenile, (*b*) adult (p. 62), 3. *P. semicirculatus;* (*a*) juvenile, (*b*) adult (p. 62), 4. *Pomacanthus arcuatus;* (*a*) juvenile, (*b*) adult (p. 63), 5. *P. paru;* (*a*) juvenile, (*b*) adult (p. 63)

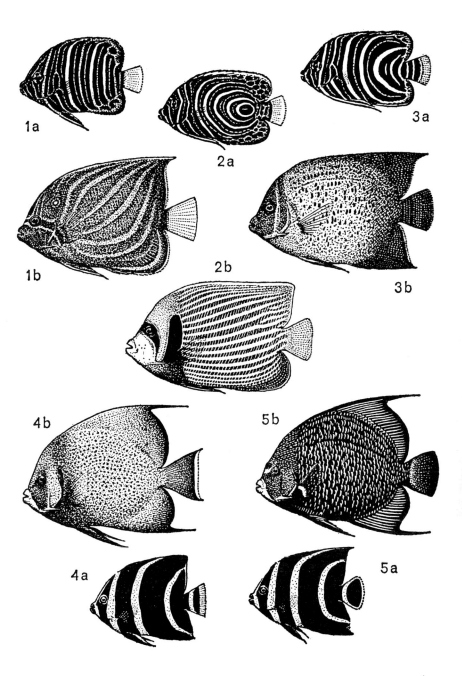

Color illustration 45. *Pomacanthus paru,* French angelfish, juvenile. Photo by W. Hoppe.

Illustration 46. *Pomacanthus imperator (Pomacanthodes imperator),* emperor angelfish, juvenile. Photo by Yasuda and Hiyama.

Color illustration 47. *Pomacanthus paru,* French angelfish, adult.

Color illustration 48. *Pomacanthus imperator (Pomacanthodes imperator),* emperor angelfish, adult. Photo by Dr. Herbert R. Axelrod.

water with protruded jaws; in the wild they browse small animals off rocks. Some will take lettuce or *Riccia*.

*Descriptions: Chaetodontoplus mesoleucus* Bloch (plate II, 11). Indian Ocean. Pale yellow, the belly silvery-white, the caudal fin yellow. Hind part of the body smoky-grey, eye-stripe black. Edge of upper and lower lips blue. In many ways similar in behaviour to the Chaetodontidae, but snaps up food like the other Pomacanthidae. Rather more difficult to keep than the following species.

*Pomacanthodes* species: juveniles blue with several white, usually alternating, broad and narrow bands; formerly regarded as separate species. All do well in captivity.

*P. annularis* Bloch, Ringed Angelfish (plate IV, 1). Indo-Pacific, 15 inches. In the transition stage from the juvenile they still have narrow vertical white lines, but with pale blue bands running up diagonally from the ventral fins. Adults have a ring in the 'temporal region', blue diagonal stripes and a brown ground colour.

*P. imperator* (Bloch), Imperial Angelfish (plate IV, 2). Indo-Pacific, 14 inches, on offshore reefs. Adults blue-green with bright yellow longitudinal stripes; eye-stripe, throat and shoulder bands black edged with white. Tail fin yellow. The juvenile form was formerly known as *P. nikobariensis*.

*P. semicirculatus* (Cuvier), Blue Angelfish (plate IV, 3). Tropical Indo-Pacific, 15 inches. Adults have a yellowish body with dark spots; head black with white lips; dorsal, caudal and anal fins blue-black with small, white spots.

## Table for the identification of the young of these three species:

| *Pomacanthodes* | *P. imperator* | *P. semicirculatus* | *P. annularis* |
|---|---|---|---|
| Forehead with: | Transverse bands | Longitudinal bands | Longitudinal bands |
| Tail fin: | | Half patterned in blue-white | Completely transparent from the root |

**Table for the identification of Pomacanthodes (contd.):**

| White body stripes: | Circular, with a closed ring in front of the caudal fin | Slightly curved | Straight |
|---|---|---|---|
| Rear of dorsal and anal fins showing: | No pattern | | Rings or half-rings |

*Pomacanthus* species: juveniles black with a few yellow transverse stripes; do well in captivity.

*P. arcuatus* (Linnaeus), French Angelfish (plate IV, 4). West Indies, 15 inches. Adults silky-grey, each scale patterned with black, the ventral fins yellow.

*P. paru* (Bloch) (plate IV, 5). West Indies. 13 inches. Adults velvety-black, the scales edged with yellow.

**Table for the identification of the young of these two species:**

| *Pomacanthus* | *P. arcuatus* | *P. paru* |
|---|---|---|
| Central yellow band ends above: | At centre of dorsal fin | At tip of dorsal fin |
| Tail fin | Back edge broad and glassy, in front of which a black and then an almost straight yellow band. | Back edge narrow and yellow. Centre black with a curved yellow band at root of fin, which extends round to the back edge to form a ring. |

Color illustration 49. *Pomacanthus semicirculatus (Pomacanthodes semicirculatus),* blue angelfish, juvenile. Photo by Yasuda and Hiyama.

Color illustration 50. *Pomacanthus semicirculatus (Pomacanthodes semicirculatus),* blue angelfish, adult. Photo by H. Hansen.

Color illustration 51. *Holacanthus bermudensis (Angelichithys isabelita)*, juvenile. Photo by Dr. Herbert R. Axelrod.

Color illustration 52. *Holacanthus bermudensis (Angelichthys isabelita)*, adult. Photo by Dr. J. E. Randall.

*Holacanthus tricolor* (Bloch) (plate V, 1), Rock Beauty. Caribbean Sea, 23 inches. Juveniles yellow with black dorsal spots edged with blue. Adults orange-yellow, head dusky yellow, flanks velvety black, edges of dorsal and anal fins red.

*Pygoplites diacanthus* (Boddaert), Royal Angelfish (plate V, 2). Pacific, 7 inches, on offshore reefs. The most brightly coloured of the marine angelfishes. Orange, with glistening white bands edged black or blue. Caudal fin pale yellow, anal fin striped violet and pink, dorsal fin purple with yellow spots, head pattern blue.

*Angelichthys* species:

*Angelichthys isabelita* Jordan & Ritter (plate V, 3). West Indies, 17 inches.

*A. ciliaris* (Linnaeus) (plate V, 4). West Indies, 23 inches.

## Table for the identification of these two species:

Juveniles: body yellow to olive, fins yellow, eye-stripes black; flank stripes narrow and white, edged with blue:

| *Angelichthys* | *A. isabelita* | *A. ciliaris* |
|---|---|---|
| Pale stripes on trunk | Straight | Curved forwards |
| Upper edge of dorsal fin | Blue only | Blue above, yellow below |
| Hind edges of dorsal and anal fins | Broad and yellow | Narrow and blue |

Adults: the dark eye-stripes and pale trunk bands have disappeared:

| *Angelichthys* | *A. isabelita* | *A. ciliaris* |
|---|---|---|
| Nape spot in front of dorsal fin | Blue only | Black with a blue ring |
| Pectoral fins | Base blue, outer edge broad and yellow | Yellow, with black at the base |

## Adults of Angelichthys species (contd.):

| | | |
|---|---|---|
| Hind edges of dorsal and anal fins | Yellow | Blue |
| Caudal fin | Only the edge is yellow | All yellow |

POMACENTRIDAE, Damselfishes
Tropical seas, in shallow water over reefs, and particularly in large coral heads. Living singly, in pairs or in groups. Diet very variable. Most closely related to the cichlids, and like the latter they have only one nostril on each side. Except for the species of *Dascyllus* and *Amphiprion* they are difficult to identify. *Abudefduf* and *Pomacentrus* have compressed teeth and the remaining genera conical ones. Usually easy to keep and long-lasting.

*Descriptions: Pomacentrus* species: operculum edge saw-like. Usually very brightly coloured, but often becoming unicoloured with age. Singly or in pairs; some spawn like the cichlids and the eggs are guarded by the pair. The majority are very aggressive towards members of their own species and to all others that are interested in hiding-places.

*P. caeruleus* (Bloch) (plate VI, 2). Indo-Pacific. Brown to bluish, with white longitudinal streaks on the scales; caudal fin yellowish-white.

*P. tripunctatus* Cuvier. Indo-Pacific, 5 inches. Blue-grey, usually with black spots edged with blue at the base of the last dorsal fin-ray or on the top of the caudal peduncle. Diagonal blue pattern particularly on the top of the head.

*Chromis* species: none of the operculum bones are saw-edged. Several, brightly coloured species, mostly living in shoals and hiding in small caves. The caudal fin is deeply forked. The hind part of the body is white or yellow, whereas the front part of body is brown, grey or blue.

*C. chromis* (Linnaeus). Common in the Mediterranean, 4½ inches. Juveniles blue-violet. Adults golden-brown, appearing blue-black at a distance, scale edges darker. Inner edges of the caudal fin white, making it appear even more deeply forked. At spawning time (July) the males settle in large groups on rocky bottoms, each fish guarding

65

Color illustration 53. *Holacanthus ciliaris (Angelichthys ciliaris),* queen angelfish, adult. Photo by *Dick Boyd.*

Color illustration 54. *Pygoplites diacanthus,* royal angelfish. Photo by Dr. J. E. Randall.

Color illustration 55. *Holacanthus ciliaris (Angelichthys ciliaris),* queen angelfish, juvenile. Photo by Dr. Herbert R. Axelrod.

Color illustration 56. *Holacanthus tricolor,* rock beauty. Photo by J. E. Randall.

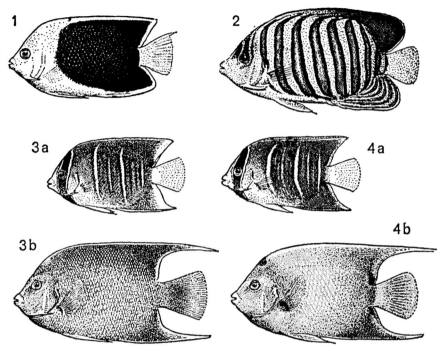

Plate V. 1. *Holacanthus tricolor* (p. 64), 2. *Pygoplites diacanthus* (p. 64), 3. *Angelichthys isabelita;* (*a*) juvenile, (*b*) adult (p. 64), 4. *A. ciliaris;* (*a*) juvenile, (*b*) adult (p. 64)

a stone. The females swim in groups, go individually to the males and attach the eggs to a cleansed stone. The males guard and fan the eggs until they hatch.

*C. xanthurus* (Bleeker). Indo-Pacific, $3\frac{1}{2}$ inches. Body and fins blue, in adults brownish. The hind parts of the dorsal and anal fins and of the caudal peduncle and fin are yellow, being paler in the adult.

Plate VI. 1. *Anthias squamipinnis* (p. 50), 2. *Pomacentrus caeruleus* (p. 50), 3. *Abudefduf saxatilis* (p. 68), 4. *A. oxyodon* (p. 68), 5. *Dascyllus trimaculatus* (p. 68), 6. *D. aruanus* (p. 68), 7. *D. reticulatus* (p. 68), 8. *D. marginatus* (p. 68), 9. *Amphiprion ephippium* (p. 70), 10. *A. melanopus* (p. 70), 11. *A. percula* (p. 70), 12. *A. akallopisos* (p. 70), 13. *A. xanthurus* (p. 70), 14. *Premnas biaculeatus* (p. 70)

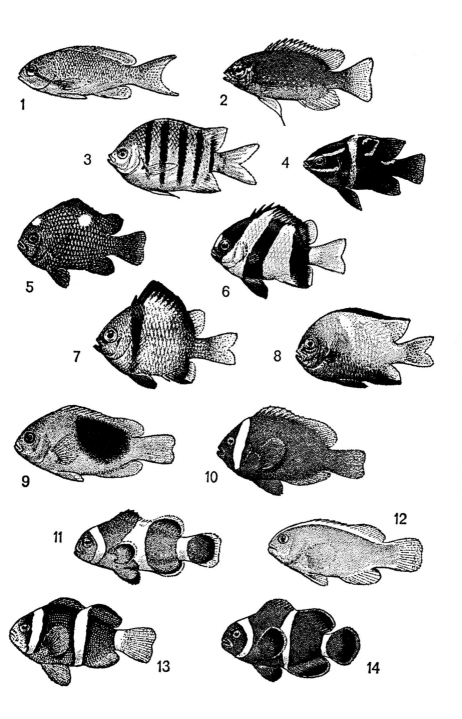

Color illustration 57. *Dascyllus albisella,* Hawaiian threespot damselfish. Photo by Herbert R. Axelrod.

Color illustration 58. *Dascyllus aruanus,* banded puller or white-tailed damselfish. Photo by Dr. Herbert R. Axelrod.

Color illustration 59. *Abudefduf saxatilis,* sergeant major. Photo by Dr. J. E. Randall.

Color illustration 60. *Dascyllus reticulatus,* reticulated damselfish. Photo by R. Allard.

*Abudefduf* species: none of the operculum bones saw-edged. Several active species in tropical waters. Usually hide in caves, crevices or among seaweeds.

*A. saxatilis* (Linnaeus) (plate VI, 3). Indo-Pacific, 9 inches. Whitish-yellow, bluish below, the bands dark to black. *A. sexfasciatus* (Lacépède) with dark bands on each caudal lobe and *A. septemfasciatus* are very similar.

*A. oxyodon* (Bleeker) (plate VI, 4). Malayan Archipelago, 4 inches, on reefs. Black, with longitudinal blue stripes and a yellow girdle which becomes narrower and paler with age.

*Dascyllus* species: only the edge of the operculum is saw-like. Small-mouthed plankton-feeders. Live in groups above clefts in coral-heads, into which they retreat when in danger. In attack and defence they produce rather loud clicking sounds. They spawn on coral branches or stony surfaces. The male shows the female the spawning place by swimming up and down, and later guards the eggs alone until they hatch. *Dascyllus* sometimes go into sea-anemones like *Amphiprion*. The species are easy to distinguish by coloration.

*D. trimaculatus* (Rüppell) (plate VI, 5). Indo-Pacific, 3 inches. Velvety-black with three pale white spots which almost disappear when the fish is scared. In spawning excitement the black changes to reddish-grey.

*D. albisella* Gill. Honolulu. Like the preceding, but the white flank spots are much larger.

*D. aruanus* (Linnaeus), Banded Puller (plate VI, 6). Indo-Pacific, 3½ inches. White with blackish-blue bands, the ventral fins blue below. Males larger than females, which have a whitish spot on the forehead. In the male the first paler band is steely blue.

*D. reticulatus* (Richardson) (plate VI, 7). Indo-Pacific, 2¼ inches. Pale yellowish-brown, scale edges dark giving a reticulate pattern, transverse bands dark brown. The hindmost band (between the dorsal and anal fins) disappears with age, and the front one probably also does so later on. Often confused with the following species.

*D. marginatus* (Rüppell) (plate VI, 8). Indo-Pacific, 3½ inches. Front part of body brown below, hind part whitish above. The soft dorsal and caudal fins glassy violet, the ventrals black, as are the edges of the dorsal and anal fins in 'captivity coloration'. For according to Abel, in the wild (at least in the Red Sea) these fish are whitish-grey in front, becoming darker towards the rear, the back from the mouth to the end of the dorsal fin is sulphur-yellow, and the ventra and anal fins are edged with dark blue.

*D. carneus* (Fischer). Tropical coasts of East Africa, $3\frac{1}{2}$ inches. Grey-brown, with two large white dorsal spots and dark brown bands between the dorsal and ventral fins. Soft dorsal and caudal fins glassy violet. When excited the head becomes dark olive, the bands almost black and the rest of the body very pale. When unwell the whole body is a sickly grey and the white spots disappear.

*Amphiprion* species, Anemone-fish. Indo-Pacific. The edges of the operculum and pre-operculum saw-like. Scales smaller than in the damselfishes. All species live among the tentacles of large actinian sea-anemones (*Discocoma, Stoichactis*, see p. 31), but vary in the degree to which they are tied to these: *A. ephippium* is often seen at quite a distance from an anemone, but *A. akallopisos* never. These fish are not immune to the poison of the sting-cells of the anemones —which prey on other fish—but they do not stimulate the sting-cells to fire. It is still not completely clear how this mechanism functions. All the species can be kept without anemones, and they will then hide in among coral branches. In attack and defence they make a 'tack-tack' sound. They form closely knit pairs, and jointly guard the eggs which are laid on a stone.

The species with more than one white transverse band are often scarcely distinguishable, and it is possible that they all belong to the same species. The young stages often have more white bands than the adults (the hindmost bands disappear), but some individuals may retain the juvenile pattern. The only species which cannot be confused with others are *A. percula* and *A. akallopisos*. *A. frenatus* Brevoort and *A. melanopus* Bleeker can be distinguished from *A. ephippium* by the coloration of the anal and ventral fins: *A. ephippium* has a pale anal and a partly pale ventral, *A. frenatus* has both fins dark at the base (or at least a dark front edge to the ventral), and *A. melanopus* has completely dark anal and ventrals. In addition, however, it is known that at spawning time the edges of the anal and ventral fins become strikingly black in the males of *A. ephippium*. So the differences between the species should be used with care. Furthermore, all three species retain a white head-band (the young also have a white body-band); but young, so-called *A. ephippium* are continually being imported, which never have even a trace of the white head-band (plate VI, 9).

Color illustration 61. *Amphiprion melanopus.* Photo by Dr. G. R. Allen.

Color illustration 62. *Amphiprion perideraion,* false skunk-striped anemone-fish. Photo by Dr. G. R. Allen.

Color illustration 63. *Amphiprion biaculeatus (Premnas biaculeatus),* spine-cheeked anemonefish. Photo by Dr. Herbert R. Axelrod.

Color illustration 64. *Amphiprion ocellaris* (*Amphiprion percula* ), clown anemonefish. Photo by Yasuda and Hiyama.

*A. akallopisos* Bleeker (plate VI, 12). 2½ inches. Pale reddish, with longitudinal white stripes on the head and along the back. No transverse white bands.

*A. perideraion* Bleeker. Sunda Archipelago to the Philippines, 2½ inches. Like the preceding but with transverse white bands on the head. Delicate in captivity.

*A. ephippium* Bloch (plate VI, 9). 4½ inches. Glowing red, the flanks with a large, irregularly defined black spot. Juveniles with white head-bands. Anal fin pale, ventrals with pale areas. Longlasting.

*A. melanopus* Bleeker (plate VI, 10). See generic description above.

*A. percula* (Lacépède) (plate VI, 11). 3 inches. The best known member of the genus. Orange-brown with white bands. Unmistakable.

*A. xanthurus* Cuvier & Valenciennes (plate VI, 13). 3½ inches. Black or dark brown, the belly sometimes paler. Three white bands.

*A. bicinctus* Rüppell has no tail-band, the body-band is narrower than the head-band and ends below in a point. Background colour black to golden-yellow (in fish without a territory). The coloration of the soft dorsal, anal and ventral fins allegedly varies within the species from yellow to black. The identification of the other similar species (*A. sebae*, *A. tricinctus*, *A. polymnus*) is rather problematical, and depends *inter alia* on whether or not the body-band extends up to the edge of the dorsal fin and whether the caudal fin has a dark centre and pale edges. Indeed one comes across individuals in which the pattern is intermediate between several species. For example, *A. xanthurus* may have a dark spot on the otherwise yellow caudal fin. The specimen shown in photographic plate II is probably a variant of *A. xanthurus* with a very pale belly and pale edges to the caudal and soft dorsal fins.

*Premnas biaculeatus* Bleeker (plate VI, 14). Indo-Australian region, 5½ inches. Velvety-black, the fin centres chestnut-brown, the bands white. The only species in the genus, which is distinguished from *Amphiprion* by having a powerful spine beneath each eye. Live in certain specific sea-anemones. At spawning time the male is pale orange, the female glowing red. Maintenance in the aquarium as for *Amphiprion*.

Numerous species particularly in warm seas, but also represented in colder regions. Body form and feeding habits very variable. The smaller species feed for preference on invertebrates living on sandy bottoms. Wrasse can easily be recognized by their method of swimming; they move by means of simultaneous back strokes of the pectoral fins, using the tail as a rudder. The closely related parrot-fishes (see p. 72) swim in the same way but they are easy to distinguish by their mouth. Some wrasse spawn in open water (*Thalassoma, Coris, Xyrichthys*), others build nests of algae or sand (*Labrus, Crenilabrus*), in which the males guard the brood. The species are very difficult to identify, because young and adults or males and females are often completely different in appearance (see p. 89).

*Descriptions: Labroides* species: Indo-Pacific, four species, in all of which a proportion of the diet consists of ectoparasites taken off other fish (see p. 102). When excited the caudal fin is spread and the tail region jerked rhythmically upwards.

*L. dimidiatus* (Cuvier & Valenciennes), Cleaner-wrasse (plate VII, juvenile and adult). Also known as *Fissilabrus*. 3½ inches. Juveniles black with blue dorsal stripes. Adults bluish-white with a longitudinal dorsal black stripe.

*Coris* species: Indo-Pacific. Nine to eleven dorsal spines.

*C. formosa* (Bennett) (plate VII, 5). 15 inches. Usually confused with *C. gaimard* (Quoy & Gaimard), although both are easy to distinguish, except during the transition to the adult stage. When young both are a conspicuous red, with white wedge-shaped areas surrounded by black, which run down from the back to end in a point. This stage was previously regarded as a separate species, *C. grenovii* Bennett, because the adults have quite a different appearance.

(*a*) Juveniles: *C. formosa* has a dark, oval spot on the dorsal fin, which is lacking in *C. gaimard*. In *formosa* the first white stripe straddles the forehead, so that its ends appear on the sides of the head, in *gaimard* this stripe runs along the forehead and is not seen from the side. In *formosa* the first white stripe on the trunk (behind the ventral fins) reaches to the belly, but in *gaimard* only to the middle of the flanks; in *gaimard* the black edges of this stripe meet below but in *formosa* they run down to the belly alongside each other. The black edges to the white areas are broader in *formosa* than in

Color illustration 65. *Coris gaimard,* red labrid, juvenile. Photo by K. Paysan.

Color illustration 66. *Coris gaimard,* red labrid, adult. Photo by Yasuda and Hiyama.

Color illustration 67. *Coris formosa,* juvenile. Photo by W. Hoppe.

Color illustration 68. *Coris formosa,* adult. Photo by K. Paysan.

*gaimard*. The anal and ventral fins and the belly are black in *formosa*, red in *gaimard*. In general, *formosa* gives the impression of being a darker blackish-red, *gaimard* a pale red. In *formosa* the caudal fin is transparent up to the dark root or peduncle, whereas in *gaimard* it has a white vertical stripe edged with black on each side at the base; also the basal parts of the rays are similarly edged.

(*b*) Transitional stage (about 3½ inches): in *formosa* the dark edges to the white areas supposedly become increasingly broader and— like the white areas themselves—more washed out. In *gaimard* these areas retreat further backwards and become smaller and smaller.

(*c*) Adults: *gaimard* has broad, blue-green (slightly wavy), almost horizontal stripes on the gill-cover, where *formosa* has no horizontal stripes. On the purplish-brown trunk, *formosa* has large black, *gaimard* small blue spots. In *gaimard* the caudal fin is dark except for the narrow terminal edge, in *formosa* the whole of the posterior half is transparent.


*C. angulata* Lacépède. Red Sea. The largest species in the genus, up to 45 inches. Juveniles whitish-grey; two black dorsal spots under-laid with bright red. Live singly near to reefs, and feed on molluscs from open stretches of sand.

*Thalassoma* species: seven to eight dorsal spines. In all oceans, very brightly coloured.

*T. bifasciatum* (Bloch), Blue-head (plate VII, 6). Caribbean Sea, 5½ inches. Males: head blue-violet, body green, transverse bands white with broad black edges. Females and juveniles: yellow, white on the belly, with dark longitudinal bands on the centre of the flanks. When in poor condition the front part of the body is brown-grey with five to six narrow, transverse white bands, the belly pale.

*Iniistius:* Indo-Pacific and Red Sea. The first two dorsal spines form a separate fin on the head. Only a single species:

*I. pavo* (Cuvier & Valenciennes) = *Xyrichthys pavoninus* (plate VII, 7). 13 inches. Pale whitish, with greenish transverse bands and a yellow anal fin, but the coloration is very variable.


SCARIDAE, Parrotfishes

Several, often very brightly coloured species in all tropical seas.

Elongated fish with large scales. Teeth fused to form a parrot-like beak. Many bite off pieces of coral and chew them (which produces quite a noise), browse algae and polyps and excrete vast quantities of fine coral-sand. Apart from the method of swimming (see p. 71) the other striking character is the more or less arched upper jaw. The genus *Sparisoma* only occurs in the Atlantic; it spawns in open water, the male and female rising to the surface while circling round each other.

*Description: Scarus taeniopterus* Desmarest (plate VII, 8). West Indies, 11 inches. Males blue, with reddish longitudinal stripes on the middle of the flanks, an orange-brown longitudinal band in the centre of the dorsal fin and on the edges of the caudal fin. Females striped greenish-brown and white, the fins yellow; until recently regarded as a separate species, *S. croicensis*.

SIGANIDAE, Rabbitfish, Spinefeet
Indo-Pacific. Slimy skin. Characterized by the sharp spine which projects forwards in the region of the nape. Sharp fin spines. Upper lip always munching. Live in shoals, grazing on algae in particular. Very active swimmers.

*Description: Siganus vermiculatus* Cuvier & Valenciennes, Vermiculated Spinefoot (plate VII, 9). Indian Ocean, 15 inches. Pale background with tortuous olive-brown markings.

ACANTHURIDAE, Surgeonfish
Distributed in the warm seas of the world. Very active swimmers, requiring plenty of space. Swim only with the help of the pectoral fins. On each side of the caudal peduncle there is a sharp spine which can be flicked forward like a scalpel or penknife; it is used as a weapon in fights between members of the same species. Vegetarians with a small mouth. At spawning time large shoals gather together at twilight, and many species are then very brightly coloured. A few fish from the big group will then swim up together for a short distance, release their sperm and eggs and dive down again (cf. *Thalassoma* and *Sparisoma*). The larvae have extremely long second dorsal and anal spines and equally long ventral spines (the acronurus stage).

*Descriptions: Paracanthurus theuthis* (Lacépède) (plate VII, 10). Indo-Pacific, 9 inches. Juveniles blue, with the flanks and edges of

Color illustration 69. *Thalassoma bifasciatum,* Bluehead wrasse, female. Photo by Dr. J. E. Randall.

Color illustration 70. *Thalassoma bifasciatum,* bluehead wrasse, male. Photo by Dr. J. E. Randall.

Color illustration 71. *Scarus taeniopterus,* princess parrotfish, female. Photo by Dr. J. E. Randall.

Color illustration 72. *Scarus taeniopterus,* princess parrotfish, male. Photo by Dr. J. E. Randall.

the caudal fin black and the caudal fin itself yellow. The older they become the more the yellow spreads forwards at the expense of the blue. The oval spot behind each pectoral remains blue and so do the dorsal and anal fin bases and the patterning on the head.

*Acanthurus xanthopterus* Cuvier & Valenciennes (plate VII, 11). East Africa to West Mexico, 18 inches. Easily the largest species in the genus. Pale grey with yellow fins; when excited the body becomes darker with four conspicuous longitudinal blue stripes on the anal and dorsal fins. (The very similar *A. mata* has eight to nine such stripes.) In 'fight' coloration, very dark with transverse white bands above the root of the tail. In nature, browses on filamentous algae growing on sandy bottoms.

*A. leucosternon* Bennett, White-breasted Surgeonfish. Indo-Pacific, 11 inches. Pigeon-blue, the face black, dorsal fin yellow, anal fin and throat white. An unmistakable species.

*Zebrasoma veliferum* (Bloch), Zebra-striped Surgeonfish (plate VII, 12). Indo-Pacific, 11 inches. Olive, the stripes on the body orange; head, throat and caudal fin with pale spots. Dorsal and anal fins very large. Live for preference in shoals and browse algae off rocks in shallow water, when the dorsal fin often sticks up above the surface.

*Naso* species have two immovable bony bucklers, each with a keel or with a rigid spine, in place of the folding knives. Some species carry a protuberance or a long horn on the forehead.

## PLECTOGNATHI

Widely distributed in all warm seas. Show a wide range of body form and specialization. The group is divided into various families: with fin spines: Triacanthidae, Balistidae, Monacanthidae, Aluteridae; without fin spines: Ostraciontidae, Diodontidae, Canthigasteridae, Tetraodontidae, Lagocephalidae. This subdivision into families varies from author to author.

Plate VII. 1. *Labroides dimidiatus;* (*a*) juvenile, (*b*) adult (p. 71), 2. *Aspidontus taeniatus* (p. 83), 3. *Runula rhinorhynchus* (p. 84), 4. *Elacatinus (Gobiosoma) oceanops* (p. 84), 5. *Coris formosa;* (*a*) juvenile, (*b*) adult (p. 71), 6. *Thalassoma bifasciatum;* (*a*) juvenile, (*b*) adult (p. 72), 7. *Iniistius pavoninus* (p. 72), 8. *Scarus taeniopterus*, female (p. 73), 9. *Siganus vermiculatus* (p. 73), 10. *Paracanthurus theuthis* (p. 73), 11. *Acanthurus xanthopterus* (p. 74), 12. *Zebrasoma veliferum* (p. 74)

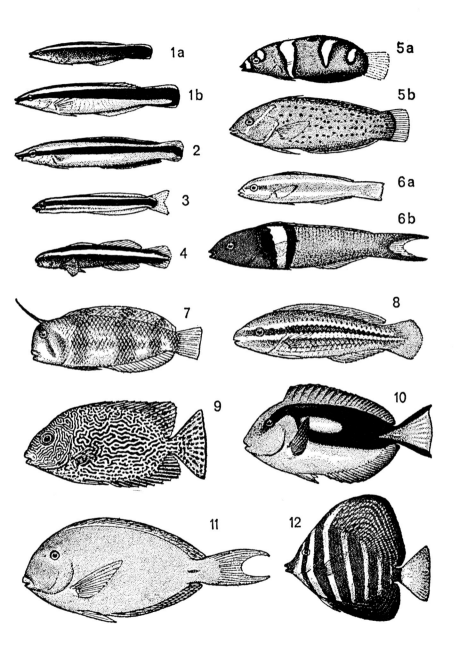

Color illustration 73. *Triacanthus biaculeatus,* spikefish. Photo by A. Norman.

Color illustration 74. *Siganus vermiculatus,* vermiculated spinefoot. Photo by K. Paysan.

Color illustration 75. *Zebrasoma desjardinii,* sailfin tang. Photo by Dr. Herbert R. Axelrod.

TRIACANTHIDAE, Spikefishes

Ventral fins modified to form long, powerful spines. First dorsal spine equally long. Open-water fish, which, as adults, swim by the snake-like movement of the tail; the undulating dorsal and anal fins are of less importance. Unmistakable.

*Description: Triacanthus* (plate VIII, 6). Silvery, often with dark spots. Caudal fin deeply forked. Easy to keep and live a long time. About 5 inches.

BALISTIDAE, Triggerfishes

In all warm seas, usually in shallow waters close to reefs. Powerful teeth, used for biting hard prey. Many have poisonous flesh. First dorsal spine very powerful and held erect with a catch articulation. Almost all the species can be kept, but they are aggressive at least to members of the same species, and often also to related forms of the same size. Many sleep lying on their side. When in danger they wedge themselves into crevices. Swim by the undulations of the dorsal and anal fins, with help from the pectorals. Prefer to search for food on sandy bottoms, where they blow water out of their mouths to wash away the sand and expose the prey. They also eat echinoderms which most other animals leave alone. Some make sandy pits for spawing, in which they guard the eggs until they hatch.

*Descriptions: Odonus niger* (Rüppell) (plate VIII, 1). Indo-Pacific, 18 inches. The only species in the genus and one of the best known triggerfishes. Blue when alive. The protruding 'chin' is quite characteristic. Wander about in packs over the reefs, diving into hiding-places when threatened. A peaceful species. When swimming fast the dorsal and anal fins flap from side to side, without showing any undulations.

*Melichthys ringens* (Osbeck). Tropical parts of all oceans, 18 inches. Similar to the preceding species. Black with the exception of the white dorsal and anal fin bases.

*Pseudobalistes fuscus* (Bloch). Indo-Pacific, Red Sea, 18 inches. Juveniles yellow with a dense pattern of dark blue lines and a black saddle spot between the eyes, at the base of both dorsal fins and on the caudal peduncle. When the fish is excited the saddle spots become increasingly larger, until finally the body is almost completely black with pale iridescent blue lines. Live singly on sandy bottoms in deeper water. Feed on hard-shelled echinoderms and tubeworms.

*Rhinecanthus aculeatus* (Linnaeus), Picasso Fish (plate VIII, 2). Indo-Pacific, 12 inches. Prefer quiet waters and a sandy bottom. Body white, head-stripes yellow and white, dorsal stripes black, belly stripes white, separated by yellow-brown. On the caudal peduncle several rows of black spines with the points curved backwards. In the aquarium they will sometimes feed avidly on pond-snails. Most likely to be confused with the following species:

*R. rectangulus* (Schneider), Belted Triggerfish. Tropical Indo-Pacific. Very similar to the preceding species, but with a black caudal peduncle and a broader black band running from the eyes through the pectorals to the anal fin.

*Balistapus undulatus* (Mungo Park), Undulate Triggerfish. Indo-Pacific, 11 inches. The only species in the genus. Green (darker when resting), with oblique orange stripes, the fin rays of the caudal, pectoral, dorsal and anal fins are also orange. Very aggressive. Will eat everything it can get hold of, whether hard or soft, including sea-urchins, snails, calcareous algae, coral fragments and even pieces taken from passing fish.

*Balistoides conspicillum* (Bloch), Spotted Triggerfish. Indo-Pacific, 18 inches. Velvety-black reticulate pattern, fin and back patterning yellow, lips orange-red, underside with large, round, white spots. Very aggressive.

*Hemibalistes chrysopterus* (Bloch) (plate VIII, 3). Indo-Pacific, 11 inches. Juveniles have the belly white up to the middle of the flanks, the back brown. Adults are all brown or, if they have a territory, are coloured exactly the opposite to the young, that is, with a brown belly and a pale back. The edge of the gill-cover has a whitish-yellow stripe which disappears or may even become black, as for example when the fish is fighting. The tail fin is edged with white, with white at the hind edge, and a pale brown wedge-shaped spot in the middle.

*Sufflamen albicaudatum* (Rüppell). Red Sea. Similar to the preceding species, but the white at the edges of the tail fin extends as a broad band along the caudal peduncle. This fish should in fact be put in the genus *Hemibalistes*, and it is doubtful whether it is even a separate species.

Color illustration 76. *Balistoides niger (Balistoides conspicillum)*, spotted triggerfish, clown triggerfish. Photo by K. Paysan.

Color illustration 77. *Balistapus undulatus,* undulate triggerfish. Photo by Herbert R. Axelrod.

Color illustration 78. *Rhinecanthus aculeatus,* Picasso fish. Photo by J. E. Randall.

MONACANTHIDAE, Filefishes
In all warm seas, particularly among vegetation. When in danger some position themselves head down among the seaweeds and they are then difficult to distinguish. They feed mainly on coral polyps. The body is leaf-like and laterally compressed. There is only a single spine on the belly, which can be erected, taking with it a ventral fold of skin. Many species are masters of camouflage, with an astonishing capacity for adapting their coloration and pattern. Easy to keep, they swim like the triggerfishes. The best known Indo-Pacific genus is:

*Description: Stephanolepis* (plate VIII, 5). The dorsal spine arises behind the centre of the eyes. Mostly small species ($2\frac{1}{2}$–9 inches). In *Amanses* the dorsal spine arises above the front edge of the eyes. In both genera the body is almost quadrangular, if one excludes the caudal fin. Related genera have a more elongated body (*Acanthaluteres, Navodon*).

ALUTERIDAE, Leatherjackets
In all warm seas, and like the preceding family mainly among sea-grass and seaweeds. The long dorsal spine arises above or even in front of the eyes (when lowered it may be almost invisible). No pelvic spine. A very elongate shape, sometimes marked with longitudinal black stripes.
*Description: Pseudalutarius* (plate VIII, 4). Swim forwards and backwards like a knife-fish, by means of the fast undulations of the very long dorsal and anal fins. Coloration usually just grey and brown. Some are fastidious about food.

OSTRACIONTIDAE, Boxfishes
In all warm seas. Hard bony plates beneath the skin, with only the tail protruding from the 'box'; when the fish is disturbed the tail is folded forwards against one side of the body. There are no ventral fins. Boxfishes swim with the pectoral, dorsal and anal fins, as though with four propellers, and they are expert at turning in a restricted space. They have a small mouth and feed on tiny invertebrates, particularly on sandy bottoms. In the aquarium they are often rather fastidious about food. Under-nourished individuals have concave flanks; the side walls of the box should be straight and vertical.
*Descriptions: Ostracion lentiginosus* Bloch, Blue Boxfish (plate

VIII, 7). Indo-Pacific, 7½ inches. Black to dark blue with pearly white spots. The males should have red on the edges of the back.

*O. tuberculatus* Linnaeus. Indo-Pacific, 15 inches. Looks like a dice when young; yellow with black spots, around which iridescent blue rings later appear. There are a few other species which look exactly the same when young, and up to now it has not been possible to identify them at this stage. We badly need information on the changes in coloration that take place when these fish grow up.

*Lactoria cornuta* (Linnaeus) = *Ostracion cornutus*, Long-horned Cowfish (plate VIII, 9). Indo-Pacific, 18 inches. Yellow to olive, the bony plates often with central turquoise—blue spots. The caudal fin becomes disproportionately large with age. Swim continuously in open water. The genus can be distinguished by the four horns, two above the eyes directed forwards and two below the anal fin directed backwards.

*Tetrosomus gibbosus* (Linnaeus) (plate VIII, 8). Indo-Pacific, 11 inches. Olive with dark spots. The body is triangular in cross-section, with spines at the base angles and at the apex of the pyramid. An unmistakable genus with a few species.


DIODONTIDAE, Porcupinefishes

Shallow parts of all warm seas, in the open water. No ventral fins. Porcupinefishes swim mainly with the help of the large, fan-like pectoral fins, helped by the dorsal and anal fins, and by the strokes of the caudal fin. Very large, movable eyes. These fish can inflate themselves with water to form a spiny ball. They ought not to be allowed to inflate themselves with air, as they often find this difficult to get rid of.

*Descriptions: Diodon hystrix* Linnaeus (plate VIII, 12).

Warm seas, 35 inches. Yellowish-olive with large brown spots; eyes iridescent greenish-blue, even above the pupil. In normal conditions the spines are folded down. Easy to keep, becoming hand-tame. In the wild they feed on hard-shelled molluscs and crustaceans.

*Chilomycterus schoepfi* (Walbaum), also known as *Cyclichthys* (plate VIII, 13). Atlantic, Caribbean Sea, 9 inches. Juveniles with a long soft horn above each eye which is bent backwards when swimming; this becomes shorter with age. Greyish-olive wavy pattern, with dark spots.

The spines are always erect.

Color illustration 79. *Arothron reticularis,* reticulated blowfish. Photo by H. Hansen.

Color illustration 80. *Paracanthurus hepatus (Paracanthurus teuthis),* blue surgeon. Photo by G. Marcuse.

Color illustration 81. *Lactoria cornuta,* long-horned cowfish. Photo by Yasuda and Hiyama.

Color illustration 82. *Odonus niger,* black triggerfish. Photo by Dr. Herbert R. Axelrod.

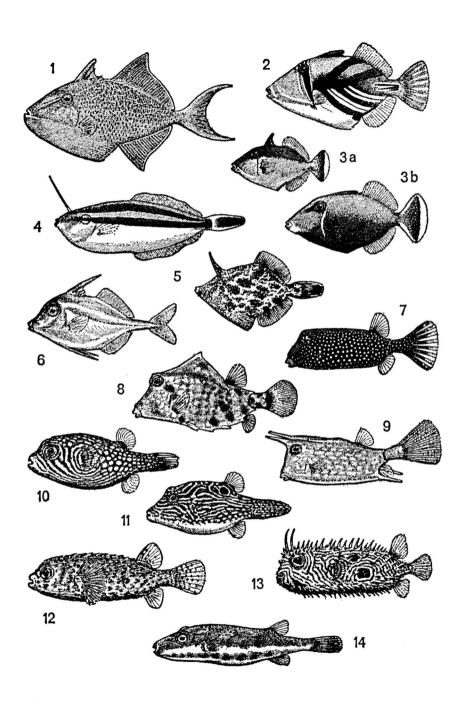

CANTHIGASTERIDAE

Warm parts of the Indo-Pacific. No ventral fins. Strikingly coloured. Method of swimming similar to that of the triggerfishes. Only a single genus.

*Description: Canthigaster margaritatus* (Rüppell) (plate VIII, 11). 5 inches. Belly whitish, back red-brown with mother-of-pearl spots. The large black eyespot at the base of the dorsal fin is characteristic of the species.

TETRAODONTIDAE, Pufferfishes

Several species in warm seas, some also in fresh water. No ventral fins. Many are poisonous. Most species can swallow a bellyful of water and thus inflate their body into a balloon. They swim like the boxfishes. The powerful beak is formed from sharp tooth plates. Only a single nostril on each side. They will eat anything living, including algae, pieces of coral, sea-squirts and sponges. Some species spawn at spring tides on the shore, the males biting hold of the tough skin of the females to anchor themselves. At least one of the fresh-water species sticks its eggs to the substrate and guards them, the pair remaining close to each other.

*Description: Arothron reticularis* (Bloch) (plate VIII, 10). Indian Ocean to New Guinea, 15 inches. Dark brown with a pale reticulate pattern on the hind body. Yellow rings around the pectoral fins and the gill openings just in front of them.

LAGOCEPHALIDAE

Like the preceding family, but the body is rather more elongated; two nostrils on each side.

*Description: Sphaeroides* (plate VIII, 14). Long, cylindrical fish, some of which lie at rest with the flattened belly on the sand, or burrow into it. Belly white, back dark brown to grey, often with a pale pattern.

Plate VIII. 1. *Odonus niger* (p. 76), 2. *Rhinecanthus aculeatus* (p. 77), 3. *Sufflamen (Hemibalistes); (a)* juvenile, *(b)* adult (p. 77), 4. *Pseudalutarius* (p. 78), 5. *Stephanolepis* (p. 78), 6. *Triacanthus* (p. 76), 7. *Ostracion lentiginosum* (p. 78), 8. *Tetrosomus gibbosus* (p. 79), 9. *Ostracion (Lactoria) cornutus* (p. 79), 10. *Arothron reticularis* (p. 81), 11. *Canthigaster margaritatus* (p. 81), 12. *Diodon hystrix* (p. 79), 13. *Chilomycterus schoepfi* (p. 79), 14. *Sphaeroides* (p. 81)

Color illustration 83. *Gobiosoma oceanops (Elacatinus oceanops), cleaner goby, neon goby.* Photo by D. Faulkner.

Color illustration 84. *Opistognathus aurifrons,* Yellowhead jawfish. Photo by G. Marcuse.

Color illustration 85. *Labroides dimidiatus,* cleaner wrasse. Photo by Dr. J. E. Randall.

Color illustration 86. *Plotosus anguillaris,* salt-water catfish. Photo by Yasuda and Hiyama.

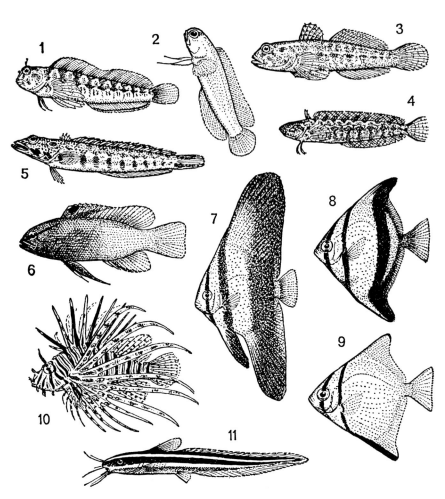

Plate IX. 1. *Blennius* (p. 83), 2. *Opistognathus* (p. 84), 3. *Gobius* (p. 84), 4. *Cristiceps* (p. 84), 5. *Parapercis* (p. 85), 6. *Gramma hemichrysos* (p. 50), 7. *Platax orbicularis* (p. 85), 8. *Monodactylus* (*Psettus*) *sebae* (p. 86), 9. *M. argenteus* (p. 85), 10. *Pterois volitans* (p. 86), 11. *Plotosus anguillaris* (p. 87)

## BLENNIOIDEA

A great number of species in warm and cold seas. Usually bottom-living fish inhabiting self-dug holes, crevices or worm tubes; on reefs they show a preference for the seaward side. Often attractively coloured, with a considerable capacity for changing colour. Swim with a snake-like movement. Predators with powerful teeth. Very intelligent (see p. 40). Easy to keep, provided each fish has its own hiding-place. Classified in several families. Identification often difficult. The female spawns on the walls or roof of the male's dwelling; the eggs are guarded by the male only. Pelagic larvae.

BLENNIIDAE, Blennies

Scaleless. Some species will voluntarily leave the water for a time to catch prey. Become hand-tame.

*Descriptions: Blennius* (plate IX, 1). Usually with tentacles above the eyes. Males larger than females, with a fleshy comb on the head during the spawning period. Very inquisitive. Aggressive towards each other. Size range (according to the species) 2–8 inches. Extremely greedy. Heavier than water.

*Petroscirtes*. Replaces the genus *Blennius* in the Indo-Pacific. Give a severe bite when picked up. Can remain completely poised in midwater, and swim like sticklebacks. Live in tubes like the following. Will eat earthworms. Peaceable with each other and with other fish. Several species have longitudinal black and yellow stripes; sabreteeth as in *Aspidontus*. The following two, closely related genera are important.

*Aspidontus*, with the species *A. taeniatus* Quoy & Gaimard, the 'Cleaner-mimic', see p. 103 (plate VII, 2). Occurrence, size and coloration as in its model, the wrasse *Labroides*. It even swims like a wrasse, using the pectoral fins, although it more frequently bends the body sideways. The ventrally placed mouth has only two large sabreteeth in the lower jaw (which can only rarely be seen) and there are two thin ventral fins, almost reduced to a single ray, of the typical blenny type. This fish can be kept successfully, even in groups; each individual lives in its own tube, which should fit it as snugly as possible and be placed somewhat above the bottom. Will feed on plankton and pieces of fish flesh, although more normally it nips off the tentacles of tubeworms and pieces of fin from other fish. Has several times been erroneously imported as a cleaner fish.

*Runula*. Closely related to *Aspidontus*. Swims with a snake-like movement. It also lives in burrows on the bottom, into which it creeps backwards like *Aspidontus*. The members of this genus are very aggressive towards each other, and so are best kept alone.

Color illustration 87. *Platax orbicularis,* orbiculate batfish. Photo by Dr. Herbert R. Axelrod.

Color illustration 88. *Platax pinnatus,* long-finned batfish.
Photo by Earl Kennedy.

*R. rhinorhynchus* (Bleeker) (plate VII, 3). Indo-Pacific, 5½ inches. Also erroneously imported as a cleaner-fish. Blue-black with yellowish-white longitudinal stripes. Mouth and teeth as in *Aspidontus*. Only eats pieces of skin from living fish or portions of the tentacle crowns of tubeworms and is therefore very difficult to keep.

*R. tapeinosoma* (Bleeker). 4½ inches. Shape as in the preceding species, flanks with transverse flecks. Similarly aggressive, but more detailed information is lacking.

CLINIDAE

Closely related to the Blenniidae but with scales.

*Descriptions: Tripterygion.* Distinguished by the tripartite dorsal fin, of which the first short, but tall, part begins on the head.

*Cristiceps* (plate IX, 4). With a normal bipartite dorsal fin. Pointed mouth. It can walk on the ventral fins. Only one species, *C. argentatus* Risso, in the Mediterranean.

*Ecsenius bicolor* Day. Indo-Pacific, 3½ inches. Steeply rising forehead. Front part of the body black, hind part and tail orange-red. The male larger and with much elongated black outer rays on the caudal fin. Should be kept in pairs, rivals will be killed. A specialized species which is very easy to keep, for it can live only on the algal growths in the tank; it will also take dried food, *Tubifex*, fish flesh, etc. It lives in burrows. The male display shows elegant seesaw movements.

OPISTOGNATHIDAE

The best known genera are *Opistognathus* and *Gnathypops* (plate IX, 2). Warm seas. Soft body with small scales. Large eyes, a large round head and a large mouth. At least some of the species occur on sand in shallow coastal waters, where they live in self-made burrows resembling wells, the edges of which they cement with stones, pieces of shell, etc. They lie in wait for small animals in the position shown in the drawing. The eyes glance around actively and the long ventral fins are spread out in front like balancing rods. When in danger they retreat back into the burrows, with the mouth agape in a threatening attitude. At least some of the species are mouth-brooders.

## GOBIOIDEA

A group with a great number of species in warm and cold seas. Always without a lateral line. Head bull-like. Ventral fins usually fused to form a suction disc. With the exception of many Eleotridae these are typically bottom-living fish, usually heavier than water, which live singly or in pairs, as described under the Blenniidae. On reefs they prefer to live on the lagoon side and in tide-pools, on temperate coasts in shallow pools. Reproduction as in the Blenniidae. Most species are easy to keep.

*Descriptions: Gobius* (plate IX, 3), the typical genus. The males make grunting sounds during the breeding season. Systematically a very confused group.

*Gobiodon* and *Paragobiodon*. Brightly coloured like coralfishes, the head attractively striped with an almost semi-circular profile. Body small and oval. The first dorsal fin with six spines. Sit hidden away among coral branches. Feed on worms and on the eggs of fish which spawn above the corals.

*Elecatinus oceanops* Jordan, sometimes placed in the genus *Gobiosoma*, Cleaner-goby (plate VII, 4). Pacific coasts, $1\frac{1}{2}$ inches. Black with bright, pale blue longitudinal stripes. Male larger than female, and with a coarser head. Behave as cleaners like *Labroides* (see p. 102). Live in groups in coral blocks, within which they probably form permanent pairs. At any rate in aquaria they will jointly guard a snail shell or similar object, in which they spawn at regular intervals, the eggs being tended by both parents. The larvae live unprotected in the plankton. This is an easy species to keep. The closely related *E. horsti* has very similar habits. They should not be put in as cleaners for predatory fish which have already become accustomed to their surroundings, otherwise they will be eaten. They should be given time to learn their environment and find a home.

PARAPERCIDAE

(Plate IX, 5). One genus: *Parapercis*. Indo-Pacific, 6 inches. Spindle-shaped bottom-living fish on sandy and rocky ground. Lie in wait for crustaceans and small fish, which they rush at from distances up to about 3 ft. The mouth is accordingly large with powerful teeth and thick lips. Small scales and a small first dorsal fin. The eyes, which are high up on the head, move about actively.

The Synodontidae (lizard-fishes) are very similar, but they have an adipose fin on the caudal peduncle (like the Salmonidae and many characins).

Color illustration 89. *Gobiodon quinquestrigatus,* five-lined goby. Photo by U. Erich Friese.

Color illustration 90. *Monodactylus sebae,* moonfish. Photo by Dr. Herbert R. Axelrod.

Color illustration 91. *Synodus* species, lizardfish. Photo by Dr. Herbert R. Axelrod.

Color illustration 92. *Monodactylus argenteus,* the Mono. Photo by Dr. Herbert R. Axelrod.

PLATACIDAE, Batfishes
Closely related to the Chaetodontidae. Indo-Pacific. Leathery-brown. The young float near the surface like large, withered mangrove leaves. Batfishes are very easy to keep, will eat large quantities of almost anything and grow incredibly quickly. These unmistakable fish require sufficient space for swimming.

*Descriptions: Platax orbicularis* Forskål (plate IX, 7). 19 inches in length, but become more than this in height! The young have dark brown transverse bands.

*P. teira* Forskål. 23 inches. Similar to the preceding species, but with very much taller dorsal and anal fins and longer ventrals, particularly in the young.


MONODACTYLIDAE, Silverfishes
Typical coastal fish, living in shoals particularly among mangrove roots. Very free-swimming. Easy to keep. The tall, silvery compressed body is quite unmistakable.

*Descriptions: Monodactylus argenteus* (Linnaeus) (plate IX, 9). Indo-Pacific, 7 inches. Unpaired fins pale yellow. The two dark transverse bands become paler with age. The tips of the dorsal and anal fins are black.

*M. (Psettus) sebae* Cuvier & Valenciennes (plate IX, 8). West coast of Africa. Like the preceding species but with taller dorsal and anal fins and the hind part of the body is darker.


SCORPAENIDAE, Scorpion-fishes
In all seas. Bottom-living fish which live singly, lurking among rocks, corals and other objects. Very bright, dappled coloration, with skin processes which help in camouflage, the colours changing according to the background. The head is large with a big mouth and numerous spines on the head bones. Predators which mainly catch living prey, particularly other fish. Some are said to be live-bearing. The body mucus is often poisonous, and a prick from the opercular spines is painful. The best known genera are *Scorpaena* and *Scorpaenopsis*, but the species are difficult to distinguish. Scorpionfishes can walk about on the thick rays on the undersides of the pectoral fins. All the twelve dorsal spines are connected by membranes. The Norway Haddock or Bergylt (*Sebastes*) from the coasts of Europe is a valuable edible fish.

86

*Pterois* species, Dragonfish or Lionfish. Similar to the preceding genera. They often hover in open water. The thirteen to fourteen long dorsal rays are not connected by membranes, and when the fish is excited they slowly oscillate from side to side, one after the other. The pectoral fin-rays are all undivided and very long, the upper ones without a connecting membrane. The head bears skin processes. About six species have been imported, but they are often just designated as *P. volitans*. All have poisonous dorsal spines, which inflict a very painful sting; in some species this is as dangerous as a cobra bite. The bite can be treated with cobra anti-venine. These are voracious fish which should be fed to satiety twice a week. They quickly become hand-tame and will then even take dead food.

*Descriptions: P. volitans* (Linnaeus) (plate IX, 10). Indo-Pacific and Red Sea, 13 inches. Striped red and white.

*Dendrochirus.* Indo-Pacific. Does not grow as large as *Pterois* (6 inches). The upper pectoral fin-rays are branched, the remainder undivided, and all are connected by a membrane. Like to hide away. Intermediate between *Scorpaena* and *Pterois*. Dark red tones predominate. Care as for *Pterois*.

*Synanceja*, Stonefish, probably the most poisonous of all fish. Live on the bottom and have the appearance of a stone covered with algae. Their habits are similar to those of *Scorpaena*.

TRIGLIDAE, Gurnards

In all except the very cold seas. The head is large with a sharply rising front and big eyes on the upper edges. Pectoral fins large and often brightly coloured on their upper sides. Gurnards live on the bottom and can 'walk', using the free lower rays of the pectoral fins which are movable like fingers and carry taste organs; the latter help the fish to find prey in the sand.

PLOTOSIDAE

Elongate body without scales. Four pairs of barbels. The young, in particular, live in large shoals on reefs with growths of algae. The genus *Plotosus* is unmistakable.

*Description: Plotosus anguillaris* (Bloch) (plate IX, 11). Indo-Pacific, 27 inches. Brown to black with whitish longitudinal stripes, which become less conspicuous with age. These fish, which should be kept in groups, are active by night, when they will clean the tank

Color illustration 93. *Dendrochirus zebra,* zebra lionfish. Photo by D. Faulkner.

Color illustration 94. *Parapercis multifasciatus,* barred perch. Photo by Yasuda and Hiyama.

Color illustration 95. *Synanceja verrucosa,* stonefish. Photo by G. Marcuse.

bottom of food remains. There are sharp, toothed spines on the dorsal and pectoral fins which may cause dangerous wounds. These fish should not be caught up in a net, as the spines penetrate the mesh; this abrades the fin membranes which are difficult to heal; the spines may fall off and some specimens will then die.

APODES, Eels and Moray-eels
Moray-eels live in holes on reef and cliff faces. No ventral and pectoral fins, the nostrils developed into small, protruding tubes, the mouth deeply split, the gill-slits small and circular and positioned far back on the head. They are often fastidious feeders, but also aggressive. Some species become very large (6 feet or more). Not really suitable for a home aquarium. The bite is poisonous.

SYNGNATHIDAE, Pipefishes and Sea-horses
These fish should be kept alone.
*Description: Hippocampus*, Sea-horses. Tropical and temperate seas. A description is surely unnecessary. The tank should be provided with thin, wiry twigs which serve as anchoring places. Sea-horses feed the whole time and only on large plankton which they chase rather unwillingly (*Corethra, Daphnia*, water-slaters, small guppies). See p. 15 for information on breeding. The fully formed young leave the paternal brood-pouch after about twelve days.
*Syngathus*, Pipefishes. These should be kept in the same way as the sea-horses.

PEDICULATI
Specialized fish which usually lurk on the bottom waiting for prey. The fishing-rod formed from the first dorsal fin-ray, which sits very far forwards on the head, is used to entice the prey. Predators, usually with large mouths. The pectoral fins, which look rather like arms, are positioned far back on the body. The ventral fins, which are similar, are positioned far forwards on the throat. The fish use these four fins like quadrupeds, to move along the bottom. All are difficult to keep for any length of time. Many species will only take live fish and are prone to infection with *Ichthyophonus*. They lay eggs, even in aquaria, in long mucous strands which float in the water. Some deep-sea anglerfishes have parasitic dwarf males. The specimens occasionally imported belong to the following families:

Body soft and dorso-ventrally flattened,
mouth large . . . . . . . . . Lophiidae (*Lophius*)
Body hard and dorso-ventrally flattened,
mouth small . . . . . . . . . . Ogcocephalidae
Body not dorso-ventrally flattened . . . . . Antennariidae
       skin rough . . . *Antennarius*
       skin soft . . . . *Histrio*

*Descriptions: Antennarius* species, often with strange shapes and coloration, live in warm seas.

*Histrio*, Sargasso Fish. 6 inches. There is only a single species, *H. histrio* (Linnaeus) which is found in all tropical seas, living among drifting seaweed, which its pattern and coloration match incrediby well.

## Alas, more unavoidable complications

Today, the fishes as a group contain more species and individuals than all the other classes of vertebrates put together. Even if one excludes the freshwater fish and those which are unsuitable for aquaria, there still remains—in theory—a vast number of other marine fish. And even the small percentage of these actually imported offers sufficient scope for trouble. There are several reasons for this:

First, many marine fish are far more highly specialized than freshwater fish (as already mentioned on p. 12), and unfortunately this applies even to the different sexes and age groups of a single species. Unless one can follow the transformations it is extremely difficult to find out who really is who. It is only when a large number of specimens are available that one can build up a complete series, from which one might, for example, discover that the fish classified in the genus *Tholichthys* are actually the larval stages of the Chaetodontidae or that the genus *Acronurus* contains the larvae of surgeonfish (Acanthuridae). And unless one can observe the reproductive behaviour it is also difficult to sort out which are the males and females of a given species for they are often very different in appearance.

Recently the six species of *Ostracion* (boxfish) have been investi-

Color illustration 96. *Histrio histrio,* sargassum fish. Photo by Dr. Herbert R. Axelrod.

Color illustration 97. *Antennarius striatus,* striped angler, toadfish. Photo by K. Paysan.

Color illustration 98. *Gymnothorax kidako,* moray eel. Photo by Yasuda and Hiyama.

gated in great detail—and the result is that there are now only three. Of course, this also happens with freshwater fish but not to the same extent; in recent years the number of parrotfish species has been reduced from three hundred and fifty to eighty! The same kind of thing is happening with the wrasse: for a long time the young of *Coris gaimard* were named *Coris grenovii*; the fish described in books as *Thalassoma nitidum* are really the females and young of *Thalassoma bifasciatum* (see p. 72); *Gomphosus varius* is the female of *Gomphosus tricolor*; *Stethojulis renardi* is the adult male of *Stethojulis strigiventer*, and so on. Reinboth has even shown that in the Mediterranean there are not two species of *Coris*, but only one in spite of the fact that biologists have recognized ripe males of both species, and ripe females of at least one. The species *Coris julis* (L) has in fact two completely different kinds of functional male; one is brightly coloured and has always been known as *Coris julis*, the other is more drably coloured, like the female, and has been called *Coris giofredi*. The curious thing about this story is that all the brightly coloured males have originally been females which have changed their sex (as sometimes happens with Swordtails), and that the males which start as males are very inconspicuous and externally indistinguishable from the females.

Many keys for identification also provide a further source of confusion. It should be realized that these are normally made for the day-to-day use of fish specialists in museums who have to compare alcohol or formalin-preserved specimens from old and new collections. What they are really using is an identification key for formalinized corpses. The aquarist is in a more favourable position, because he has the living fish in front of him, and can see much more. But the additional points he sees may not help him; in fact he only sees rather different things. For example, the method of swimming, feeding, fighting and so on, but not the number of teeth in the jaws or the shape of the gill arches. But he must know these facts if he is to use an identification key. And even if the aquarist does see more, he is not necessarily any better off. For example, it is hopeless for him to try and identify the blennies in the genus *Ecsenius* while they are still alive, because the identification key asks whether the fish are unicoloured or whether they have pale transverse bands on the head or caudal peduncle. Now what the museum ichthyologist cannot know is that they have no pale bands when at rest, but do have such bands on the head when defending a territory, and that after losing a fight the bands also appear on the body as far back as the caudal peduncle; during courtship display they sometimes even have dark bands on the caudal peduncle. So, to his astonishment the aquarist can observe one species changing into another, and then back again. He cannot know which of the bands remain when the fish is preserved in formalin—and he usually does not want to find out.

He and the museum ichthyologist are simply talking different languages; the aquarist asks himself why the beautiful blue *Odonus* is called *niger* which means 'black'. In formalin, of course, it is black and nobody realizes that in life it is really blue.

In this dilemma only a careful study of the living animal can help, so that one gradually acquires an ever-increasing catalogue of its characteristics. This is more or less the exact opposite of what the well-known naturalist Peter Artedi laid down as a guiding principle about 1735: 'Ichthyology is a science which first of all assigns names to all the parts of fishes, and from this establishes the true generic and specific names, and then occasionally remarks upon deserving characteristics. The latter, however, should be done quite briefly and concisely, because in ichthyology, as in other fields of natural history, rambling and lengthy descriptions of habits and characteristics are unprofitable, since the true and natural method of identifying animals according to genus and species must be the sole and urgent task of natural history.'

Nowadays most biologists would acknowledge that this 'urgent task of natural history' is best achieved by paying some attention to the 'habits and characteristics'; and it is the primary duty of the aquarist and of the enthusiastic diver to pass on their knowledge of these habits and characteristics. Unfortunately, this does in fact require lengthy descriptions, because an animal's threat and court-ship behaviour cannot be expressed so concisely as a tooth or fin formula. It is only when we have acquired and sorted out these descriptions that we will probably have available a usable identifica-tion key for living animals, which only asks questions concerning easily visible characters, albeit of the most varied type. And, as experience in a few small groups has already shown, we will then come considerably nearer to a natural arrangement 'of animals according to genus and species' that is based on relationships.

Color illustration 99. *Pterois volitans,* lionfish, turkeyfish. Photo by Dr. J. E. Randall.

Color illustration 100. *Hippocampus guttulatus,* Mediterranean sea horse. Photo by H. Hansen.

# Can marine fish be bred?

Of course they can. But experience to date shows that this is very difficult. Hitherto, breeding successes have been very few, and some have been purely accidental; they provide evidence that it is possible to breed marine fish, but it is not profitable, and there is no likelihood (or danger) that the offspring will affect the import of or lower the price of coralfish.

The difficulties encountered in breeding coralfish are only to a small extent connected with the problem of keeping the adults. Let us first disregard the large forms (*Platax*, *Plotosus*, etc.), for which the ordinary aquarium tank is too small. But most tanks are also too small for breeding Pomacanthidae, because they are very solitary and will only tolerate the presence of their mate. One could, I suppose, work out the improbability of two imported fish, which have cost the aquarist a lot of money, being of opposite sexes. To be sure of obtaining a pair he would need to have seven to ten fish. But quite apart from cost he would be up against the question of space, because even the smaller Pomacanthiidae will ruthlessly protect very large territories against members of their own species. The aquarist should therefore import properly mated pairs. For the same reasons the formation of pairs in the larger triggerfishes (Balistidae) is pure chance.

From the viewpoint of breeding in the aquarium we can first of all exclude all species with pelagic eggs, that is, with eggs that float free in the water, because they either stick to the walls of the tank and succumb to fungi or they are eaten by the other occupants of the tank (sea-anemones, crustaceans and so on as well as fish) and also they get trapped in the filter. Although it is true that these difficulties could be overcome, it is nevertheless not advisable to start with such species. Almost all groups of marine fish have species which produce pelagic eggs, but these also have relatives which lay adhesive eggs.

For a first attempt at breeding there are many small species, of which several individuals can be kept together in a large tank, and which in some way or other attach their eggs and may also tend them, keeping them clean and healthy.

There are however other hazards involved in breeding marine fish in the aquarium, particularly as regards the feeding of the newly hatched young. There are several marine fish which protect their brood, and also some which form permanent pairs. But we know of none which extend the period of brood protection beyond the larval or earliest juvenile stages, as is done by certain fresh-water fish, such as the Bowfin (*Amia*), the Arapaima, the catfish *Ameiurus* and many cichlids. Perhaps the advantage of having small pelagic larvae, which distribute themselves far and wide, is so great that no species will abandon this method. But, of course, pelagic larvae have to feed on tiny pelagic or planktonic organisms, and it is usually not possible to have these in a tank, because the aquarist is bound to filter off anything causing cloudiness, including the food of the planktonic organisms. Nevertheless these difficulties can be overcome as is shown by the following example.

M. Casimir and Dr H. Herkner have described (*Aquarien- und Terrarien-Zeitschrift*, vol. 15 (1962), pp. 141–4) how they succeeded in rearing *Blennius pavo* in the aquarium. For this they were fortunate in having a marine tank with a pale green 'bloom' of algae, in which there were numerous protozoans and other small organisms, up to the size of crustacean nauplius larvae. At first the newly hatched *Blennius* larvae remained motionless at the water surface, but they soon started to sink and after ten days they were drifting about in mid-water. As always happens, several of the young died between the twelfth and fifteenth day, but some went on developing. At an age of three weeks they were hunting for copepods and at four weeks, when they were about $\frac{3}{8}$–$\frac{5}{8}$ inch long, they suddenly sank to the bottom and started to eat whiteworms. In this case, the water was cloudy from natural causes, but this state of affairs can also be produced artificially.

For instance, Otto Koenig, the Director of the Wilhelminenberg Biological Station near Vienna, succeeded in rearing some *Amphiprion* from the eggs. The parents attach the eggs close together on a rock in the vicinity of their home anemone and tend them for five to seven days at 27–28°C (82–82°F), until they hatch. This happens regularly at night. At this stage the larvae ($\frac{1}{8}$ inch long) only have a very small yolk-sac. They swim towards the surface with a tumbling movement, frequently sinking again for short distances. By noon on their first day of life the yolk-sac reserve is fully expended and they then swim free in the water, searching for the very tiniest food. This is why it is so difficult to get them through the following two days.

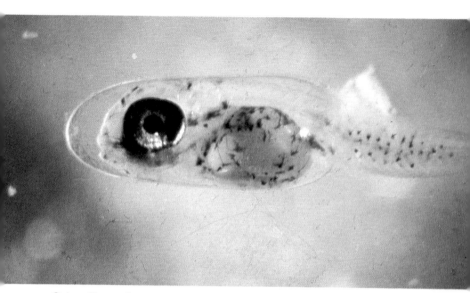

Color illustration 101. *Amphiprion* fry emerging from egg. Photo by P. Fankbonner.

Color illustration 102. *Amphiprion* nest of eggs. Photo by Dr. G. R. Allen.

Color illustration 103. Tiny sea horses leaving the brood pouch of the male sea horse. Photo by Yasuda and Hiyama.

Using a glass scoop, Koenig transferred his larvae into 8–10 inches depth of water above the grit in the tank's filter chamber. It is essential to illuminate the filter chamber because *Amphiprion* larvae will not feed in semi-darkness. At night they sleep at the surface, often lying on one side, so the air above the water should be kept warm. So long as the light is good the larvae will feed almost continuously, and he found that a broth made according to the following recipe was avidly consumed:

Mix together sea water, mussel flesh, egg-yolk, some blood-, fish- and bone-meal, dried shrimps, grated silk-worm pupae, dried cod-liver-oil, germinating wheat, fresh oatmeal, Vitamins A, $B_1$, $B_2$, $B_{12}$, D and T, nicotinamide and chlorophyll. The mixture should be passed through a sieve and stored in a refrigerator.

This broth will appear greenish and smell slightly of oatmeal. When required for use a small quantity should be brought up to the tank temperature and carefully added to the rearing tank until the water is just cloudy. The *Amphiprion* larvae will feed on this soup until they are quite replete. The filter should be kept running the whole time, and in about twenty to thirty minutes the unconsumed portion of the broth will have been removed. As soon as this happens the fish can be fed again. This food which is concocted in the same kind of way as the artificial food for hummingbirds, probably contains some superfluous items but it is certain that the oatmeal and the vitamins are particularly important.

At an age of three to four days the young *Amphiprion* are already darkly pigmented and have iridescent blue dorsal stripes. They can then deal with the smallest *Artemia* nauplii. But it is also essential to feed the brine-shrimps on the broth described above, otherwise they will very quickly become empty husks and the fish will go hungry. As the fish grow they can be offered correspondingly larger food. At four to five weeks they look roughly like their parents, but the banding is still scarcely apparent.

Probably one of the easiest marine fish to breed in the aquarium is the Dwarf Sea-horse, *Hippocampus zosterae*. But of course these only live in nature for about two years and often enough the aquarist buys them when they are one year and eleven months old. They should be fed almost exclusively on brine-shrimps, although there is no harm in offering them other live foods from time to time. The newly born young will eat freshly hatched brine-shrimp larvae that are less than twenty-four hours old. This is best done by simply strewing brine-shrimp eggs on the surface of the tank water. The empty egg-cases and any infertile eggs should be regularly removed. Here again it is an advantage to fill the brine-shrimp larvae with the nutrient broth already described or with a simplified version of it, before using them for feeding.

With a little imagination and good luck the aquarist may be able to discover other methods of rearing young coralfishes. The search will pay, for he will be treading new ground.

# A fish which mates with itself

Among the marine fish there are several very strange specialists. For instance, the anglerfishes which have developed part of the dorsal fin to form a fishing-rod for luring their prey, and useful limbs from the paired fins for crawling about. The deep-sea anglers have bizarre, brightly lit lanterns and dwarf males, which not only bite hold of the females—as male boxfishes do—but even become fused to them. The mudskippers (*Periophthalmus*) have developed into 'above-water fish', the sea-horses are the only fish which have a prehensile tail, and there are many more examples. Here I will restrict myself to mentioning a few of the breeding specialists.

The special methods of brood protection and care found in fresh-water fish also occur in the sea: sticklebacks and some wrasse (*Crenilabrus* in the Mediterranean) build nests; *Careproctus* species, Far Eastern relatives of the European *Liparis*, lay their eggs with the help of a long ovipositor under the carapace of the Kamchatka stone-crab, in much the same way as the European Bitterling lays in pond mussels.

The following specialists which are rather easy to keep may be of interest to the aquarist. The cardinal fishes (*Apogon*) and the well-builder fishes (Opistognathidae) which are usually only about 3 inches long are as a rule mouth-brooders; they carry the large balls of spawn in their mouths, which quite often can no longer be closed. Which parent broods the eggs appears to vary according to the species. The main points about sea-horses have already been mentioned (p. 19);

Color illustration 105. Unlike deep-water coral forms, corals living in shallow waters contain symbiotic algae in their tissues. Photo by Dr. Herbert R. Axelrod.

Color illustration 104. Green algae in the mantle of the giant clam *Tridacna* presumably contribute to the nutrition of the clam. Photo by Dr. Herbert R. Axelrod.

the female lays eggs in a special brood-pouch on the male, from which the completely formed young hatch out. In general, the pipe-fishes do the same, although some (e.g. *Nerophis*) carry the eggs attached to the belly but not in a pouch, in much the same way as the fresh-water catfishes of the family Aspredinidae, in which the eggs are attached to skin processes on the belly of the female.

The small surfperches (Embiotocidae) from the northern Pacific are live-bearers; some species surpass all other viviparous fish (with the exception of the Goodeidae, a family of live-bearing toothcarps), in that the young males are already sexually mature at birth. It is remarkable that these fish, which are quite easy to keep, are never seen in marine aquaria in Europe.

Equally remarkable reproductive habits are seen in one of the sea bass, *Centropristis striatus*, a member of the family Serranidae. Most of the young individuals are females, but at an age of about five years many of these change into functional males; as is well known a similar sex reversal occurs in Swordtails. But the Belted Sandfish *Serranellus subligarius* (about 5 inches long) is permanently male and female at the same time, that is, it is a hermaphrodite. At spawning time each animal possesses both ripe sperms and eggs. Normally several of these spawn together, although it is still not clear whether one functions as a male and the other as a female, or whether they all produce both sperms and eggs. Dr Eugenie Clark has, in fact, kept mature specimens in isolation and even these spawned—and the eggs developed into normal larvae. The isolated fish had produced ova which were fertilized by their own sperms, so in theory they do not require a partner. This is another case where aquarium observations would be valuable.

# Biological specialities

So far nobody has managed to count the number of different animal species—from protozoans to fish—that occur on an area of coral-reef; on the Great Barrier Reef of Australia there are estimated to be over three thousand. This wealth of species in a very restricted space necessarily leads to particularly close relationships between different animals. Naturally some relationships between different species are permanent; here I would like to mention some special or strange examples of biological speciality and describe how they are kept in the aquarium. For faced with some particularly bizarre relationship, certain uninitiated persons have been known to dismiss it as quite impossible: 'it don't exist!'

The biological terms symbiosis, mutualism, inquilism, commensalism, parasitism or mimicry can only be used to cover a few of these cases of special relationships between different species; indeed these terms are scarcely of use for our purpose, because we want to know what actually happens in a given case and not just what the relationship can be called.

Many lower animals (sponges, turbellarians, echinoderms), have single-celled algae living in their tissues, as does the common fresh-water *Chlorohydra*. These algae, which are modified green or yellow flagellates, are known as zoochlorellae and zooxanthellae. Like most other plants they are capable of photosynthesis, that is, they can harness light for the construction of organic substances, which are then used by their hosts. Animals which house these algae in their tissues have at least parts of their bodies coloured green and they require plenty of light. A good example is the European opelet anemone, *Anemonia sulcata*, which has such algae in the tentacles. When adult (with a weight of 5 cwt.) the well-known giant clam *Tridacna* is said to be nourished only on decaying zooxanthellae. Such one-celled algae live even in the skin and teeth of some fish. There are even seaweeds (*Ectocarpus*, *Cladophora*) on the teeth of parrotfishes.

Other one-celled organisms and fungi live in many animals, and even in and on fish; for examples, the notorious parasites *Ichthyophthirius* and *Ichthyosporidium* which will be discussed in the chapter on disease (see p. 104).

Some remarkable associations have developed in the sea owing to

Color illustration 106. Note the protective coloration of a gobiesocid fish, *Lepadichthys,* associated with a feather star. Photo by Dr. V. G. Springer, courtesy of the Smithsonian Institution.

Color illustration 107. A sponge crab almost hidden by the cluster of living sponges on its back. Photo by R. Straughan.

Color illustration 108. Porcelain crab *Petrolisthes* living among the tentacles of the giant sea anemone *Stoichactis*. Photo by U. Erich Friese.

the fact that the demand for space is greater than the supply. Hydroid polyps live on all kinds of firm objects, even on gorgonians, bristle-worms, crustaceans, snails and pelagic fish. Barnacles, which are crustaceans, settle on rocks and wooden piles, and also on oysters, crustacean carapaces, sponges, jellyfish, fish, turtles and whales. The small bivalve *Enterovalva semperi* fixes itself by means of a specialized adhesive foot on to the holothurian *Protankyra*; the bivalve genus *Vulsella* occurs only in living sponges, and has done so since the Tertiary, as we know from the fossil record.

The bristle-worm *Podarke pugettensis* lives in the central grooves on the undersides of starfishes, and some of its relatives take up lodgings, quite uninvited, in the 'snail house' of a hermit-crab. Animals with a home of their own are very popular. The gephyrean *Urechis* builds a U-shaped tube in the sand, in which the small goby *Clevelandia* lives, and also—usually in pairs—the crab *Scleropax*. The little bivalve *Cryptomya* occurs in the wall of the tube. The host, *Urechis*, sits at the entrance to its home tube like a piston in a cylinder; it deposits a mesh of slime around the walls of the tube entrance and then, by pumping movements of its body, sucks water through this network. The tiny organisms in the water become entangled in the slime. (The common midge *Chironomus* does much the same thing.) A small scaleworm *Hesperonoe* sits alongside the *Urechis*, taking care that it is not caught up by the pumping movements. When the *Urechis* stops pumping, in order to swallow the slimy meshwork and its contained food, the scaleworm snaps up a fragment of the slime in front of the very nose of its host.

The tiny snails of the family Pyramidellidae all live parasitically, some again on polychaetes (bristle-worms), as for instance *Chrystallida* on sabellarians (see p. 34) and *Odostomia* on *Pomatoceros*. On account of their highly specialized habits these small snails are almost unknown, although they are quite common on the coasts of Europe. They live in the entrance to the tube of their host worm. As soon as the worm emerges and spreads its tentacles to catch plankton, the extremely long proboscis of the snail starts to feel in among the tentacles; at the first movement the worm withdraws a little, but the snail is so careful, that the worm is soon at ease again. The snail's proboscis then travels along the tentacles and penetrates the worm's mouth, to suck out the 'stomach' of the peacefully feeding worm, or it may pierce its body and lap up the body tissues.

Associations involving the sharing of a home may however be advantageous to both parties. Gobies, particularly of the genus *Cryptocentrus*, very often live together with prawn-like crustaceans of the genus *Alpheus*. The crustacean digs its burrow in rather loose sand and the goby moves in; as a lodger it gets its food nearby or performs guard duties, that is, it sits in front of the hole, while the crustacean digs away, and retreats into it when danger threatens. It simply runs the crustacean down, but the latter is content to suffer this until the goby has again taken up its look-out and thus shown that the coast is clear. The extent of the mutual service and the closeness of the partnership varies from case to case. *Typhlogobius californiensis* which lives in pairs with the crustacean *Callianassa* is colourless and blind and completely dependent on the crustacean whose burrow it never leaves.

Some crabs carry sponges and sea-squirts on their carapace—to their mutual advantage. Several sea-anemones sit perched on crab carapaces or on the shells of snails and hermit-crabs.

The female of the small crab *Harpalocarcinus* sits in the fork between two branches of the coral *Pocillopora*, and allows the branches to grow over it, so that finally it remains for the rest of its life in a gall-like chamber, with openings for wafting in water and food.

There are also several fish that occupy a territory, without being permanently fixed. A good example is the well known Pilot Fish *Naucrates*, to whom giant rays or mantas are simply pieces of moving cliff face without the presence of competitors. The remarkable razorfish (*Aeoliscus*) live mostly in underwater caves. But on sandy bottoms where there are no rocks with holes they live among the long spines of the sea-urchin *Diadema*, which is common on flat sandy areas in the Indian Ocean and Red Sea. Other fish also live sheltered between its spines, particularly cardinal fish (Apogonidae), just as damselfish (*Dascyllus*) live among the branches of *Acropora* corals. When the sea-urchin starts to move off the cardinal fish follow. And if one breaks off a coral head inhabited by damselfish and swims about with it, the fish will follow closely.

Off the Palau Islands a black suckerfish (family Gobiesocidae) with yellow longitudinal stripes on the flanks lives on the arms of the feather-star *Comanthus*, together with a prawn and a bristle-worm which have the same protective coloration.

It has been known for even longer that relatives of the cardinal

Color illustration 110. Damselfish *(Dascyllus)* also seek the protection of sea anemones. Photo by Yasuda and Hiyama.

Color illustration 109. Anemone fish *(Amphiprion)* in contact with the tentacles of a giant sea anemone.

fish live in the mantle cavity of certain large marine gastropods (*Strombus*) and that the fish *Fierasfer* inhabits certain bivalves and sea-cucumbers.

However, perhaps the best known association is that between anemone-fish in the genus *Amphiprion* and some of the giant sea-anemones (*Stoichactis, Discosoma*), both of which can be kept in aquaria. Further information on this association is given under the description of anemone-fish (p. 69). But it is not only *Amphiprion* which can live unhurt among the stinging tentacles of large sea-anemones. In the wild, *Dascyllus, Thalassoma* and others do this, particularly when they are young. In the Mediterranean many individuals of the goby *Gobius bucchichii* have 'their own' opelet anemone (*Anemonia sulcata*), into which they retreat without being damaged when danger threatens. Abel has shown that the goby is protected so long as its body is covered by a good healthy layer of mucus. The spider-crab *Stenorhynchus phalangium* often sits beneath the tentacles of the same species of sea-anemones.

It often happens that more than two different species live together. Thus, in the Palau Islands, a small red goby lives on the thin stems of the coral *Junceella* and when frightened moves up and down its own stem, but never goes on to the neighbouring stems, however close they may be. Feather-stars (crinoids) perch higher up, usually entwining several stems. Among the arms of the feather-star live a starfish and another spider-crab (*Harrovia*).

The small prawn *Periclimenes pedersoni* always sits below or on the sea-anemone *Bartholomaea annulata*, which is evidently popular as a protector, because other crustaceans (*Heteromysis, Alpheus, Stenorhynchus*) and even fish—a *Paraclinus* and a cardinal fish—also live in association with it. *Periclimenes* is a cleaner-prawn, which lives in loose symbiosis with fish, as do other cleaners.

# The trade of cleaner

There are great numbers of parasites in the sea although none of these are insects, for here their 'niche' is occupied by crustaceans and these are just as troublesome. Fish in particular often find it extremely difficult or even impossible to get rid of skin parasites. It is true that many perch-like fish, including surgeonfish, can wipe their eyes, the sides of their heads and the flanks with the pectorals, so far as these fins reach; some elongated blennies wipe their head by turning the tail fin forwards—but large parts of the body remain unscratchable. Fish living near the bottom will scrape themselves on sand or firm objects, but with the well known scarcity of free space on the bottom these sites are usually occupied—only too often by spiny, nipping or stinging animals. Open-water fish have even more difficulty; they rub themselves against each other or against the rough flanks of sharks, they jump out of the water and flop back again or swim quickly through patches of flotsam.

So it is no wonder that animals of the most different species—the so-called cleaners—have become specialized for hunting and eating these troublesome parasites, a form of mutual help. This must be a successful trade, for among the relatively few marine animals whose habits are adequately known, over twenty-five fish species from eight families, six prawns or shrimps, one crab and a worm practise cleaning as their main or subsidiary occupation.

Unfortunately we still do not know much about the cleaner-fish of colder seas, except that they usually wander around in groups and follow other fish to clean them. In the tropics the cleaners are more specialized and better known, and characteristically this has impressed itself on simple observers who reflect the position in the popular names that they use; to the Mexican fishermen in the Gulf of California the angelfish *Holacanthus passer* is often known as 'el barbero' (the barber) and the West Indian prawn or shrimp *Stenopus hispidus* is called the barber-shop shrimp.

The cleaners often carry out their job in pairs. They usually have a permanent home on the reef and the customers come to them. One can take the comparison further and speak of those with regular customers and those with chance customers. The first have their own fixed territories in the neighbourhood, the others are continu-

Color illustration 111. *Aeoliscus strigatus*, razorfish, may live among the long spines of the sea urchin *Diadema*. Photo by Yasuda and Hiyama.

Color illustration 112. *Stenopus hispidus,* Banded coral or barber-shop shrimp.

Color illustration 113. *Holacanthus passer,* passer angelfish. Photo by Dr. Herbert R. Axelrod.

ously on the move as open-water fish. Among the regular customers of the mostly small cleaners are such large predatory fish as sea-perch, snappers, dragonfish; as soon as they are in the queue they open their mouths and lift their gill covers so that the cleaner has free access. They spread their fins on whose membranes parasites are particularly wont to settle, and then remain motionless, without breathing, usually in abnormal positions in the water as though in a trance, until the cleaners have finished their work. Moray-eels are nocturnal animals; but as the barber-shops are only open during the day they will even come out in the light and allow their body and mouth to be cleaned right down into the throat. It is still not clear how the cleaners always emerge unscathed from these different jaws; they are certainly not inedible. But they do have conspicuous colour patterns although these are not all the same.

It is only the highly specialized cleaners (*Elacatinus, Labroides*) that inspect the mouths of predatory fish and remove loose skin and similar scraps of tissue from wounds on the body. Some crustaceans even make small incisions in the fish skin with their pincers—so that the customer winces but still remains motionless—and then fetch out hidden parasites.

There are several cleaners among the wrasse. First there is a complete genus of cleaners, *Labroides*, with four species: *dimidiatus* (plate VII juvenile and adult), *bicolor*, *rubrolabiatus* and *phthirophagus* (which means louse-eater). Other cleaners are *Oxyjulis californica* (the senorita of the Americans), *Bodianus rufus*, and particularly when young the Blue-head, *Thalassoma bifasciatum* (plate VII); and in the Mediterranean there are *Coris julis* and *Crenilabrus melanocercus*. The small goby *Elacatinus oceanops* which is easy to keep in the aquarium is a particularly active cleaner. Among the rarely imported cleaners are *Gramma hemichrysos* (plate IX), *Anisotremus virginicus* (plate I) which only cleans when young, and *Chaetodon nigrirostris*. Some species of Pomacanthidae, such as *Heniochus acuminatus*, also clean when young.

Almost any marine fish may act as customers for the cleaners, which will even attend to large sharks and swim in and out of the gill-slits of the admittedly harmless giant manta rays. The Pilotfish (*Naucrates*) and Remoras (*Remora*) also act as cleaners. In the aquarium it is possible to see fish actively searching for cleaners, and pressing in upon them. Or, if there are none, they will repeatedly hold up large prawns or crabs against the sides of their bodies.

It is only fairly recently that biologists have begun to realize the important role played by cleaners in the sea. C. Limbaugh and the Pederson brothers have kept so-called cleaner stations—prominent positions on the reef where several cleaners gather together—under continuous observation. Within a period of six hours of daylight they counted three hundred customers for a single cleaner-fish. As an approximation, this means that in twelve hours a hundred cleaners would attend to some sixty thousand customers, which come to this cleaner station. These divers also saw that sick and wounded fish came for cleaning several times a day. To provide further evidence Limbaugh caught up all the cleaners known to him on two small isolated reefs in the Bahamas. In a few days the number of fish in the area fell rapidly; they simply wandered away, so that the previously richly populated reefs in the vicinity were largely denuded of fish life. After two weeks there only remained a few stubborn occupiers of territories, with conspicuously damaged fins, ulcers, white fungus infections and open wounds. Later on, cleaner-prawns and young cleaner-fish came in but the old visitors to the reef did not return. On the other hand the visits of young customers did increase. From these observations it has been suggested that many very productive fishing grounds off islands, coastal shallows and wrecks are actually cleaner stations, at which deep-water and pelagic fish and also wandering shoals regularly assemble.

Finally, there is some completely different, but extremely interesting confirmation of the efficiency of the cleaners: this is the false cleaner or cleaner-mimic. Some aquarists who had obtained a *Labroides dimidiatus* from the first importation at the dealers, were in for a big surprise. Sure enough, the newly arrived cleaner approached the other fish, which—as expected—held themselves very still. But the result was completely unexpected. For the customers had soon lost pieces of fin and also their confidence in the rabid cleaner. Here the buyer, importer, exporter and catcher had all been deceived just as much as the fish which had let themselves be cleaned; the presumed cleaner was in fact a blenny, *Aspidontus taeniatus*, which surely provides the most beautiful example of mimicry. It resembles the cleaner-wrasse *Labroides dimidiatus* not only in size, form and coloration (see plate VII), but it also swims

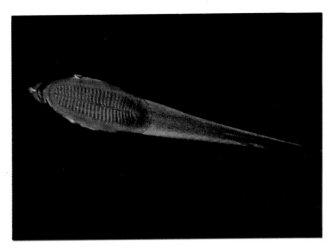

Color illustration 114. *Remora* can also act as cleaners occasionally. Photo by Yasuda and Hiyama.

Color illustration 115. *Epinephelus* with cleaner wrasses, *Labroides dimidiatus.* Photo by Yasuda and Hiyama.

Color illustration 116. *Bodianus rufus* and *Labroides dimidiatus,* cleaner wrasse. Photo by K. Paysan.

Color illustration 117. *Dascyllus albisella,* damselfish, apparently cleaning a surgeon fish, *Acanthurus.* Photo by Dr. Herbert R. Axelrod.

like a wrasse, by beating the pectoral fins, which is a completely abnormal method of progression for a blenny. It can also imitate the striking cleaner dance (see p. 71), which was first observed in the wild by I. Eibl-Eibesfeldt. The mimic even faithfully imitates local races of the cleaner—with or without black streaks at the base of the pectoral fin, with or without orange flank spots.

Here I will not enter into the many open questions surrounding this problem, which to a large extent are capable of being solved with skill and thought, nor will I cite other remarkable relationships between different species of marine animals. Take the cleaner trade as a model example and observe it with your own eyes. I should only warn you of one thing; do not always assume that conclusions reached from aquarium observations will hold in the wild. In the aquarium some highly instructive things take place, which are not however normal, that is, not typical of nature. For instance, in the Plymouth Aquarium, Wilson saw the pipefish *Entelurus aequoreus* clean a John Dory, *Zeus faber*, which even raised its gill-covers. However, one does not know at all whether the same happens in nature or whether the John Dory is normally cleaned by another fish and the pipefish has only learnt it in the aquarium. And there are other possibilities.

# Some unfortunately common diseases

*The water*

If the sea water is frothy or begins to smell it must be renewed immediately. Foam or froth is a sign of fouling, often by organic compounds.

If the sea water smells of chlorine (it may also have a greenish tint) the fish will then hang at the surface gasping. As first aid it is usually sufficient to dissolve a small quantity of sodium thiosulphate in water and stir it into the tank.

Cloudiness of the water due to bacteria can be removed in a few days if the water is intensively irradiated by an ultraviolet lamp, which kills all the germs.

*Quarantine*

Newly obtained fish should be put into a simple all-glass tank for two to three weeks; a few flowerpots, which are easy to keep clean, will provide hiding-places. The water should be well aerated; but it should only be filtered if this is compatible with any drug that has been added (see below). With tropical fish the temperature of the water can be raised (with suitable controls) to about 30°C (86°F), and this will quickly make all kinds of disease apparent.

The water can then be dosed with a heaped teaspoonful of Ectozone per 6–12 gallons. In an Ectozone bath many fish will throw off the outer layer of slime or mucus and with it many parasites; naturally the water must then be changed. Koenig recommends alternating baths of penicillin and Ectozone. For a penicillin bath use 200,000 international units of crystalline penicillin per litre (1·8 pints) of sea water, with strong aeration but no filtration. The fish should remain for not more than twelve hours in this bath, as toxic effects have been observed after twenty-four hours. For this reason penicillin baths cannot be given directly one after the other. Towards the end of the course of treatment the concentration of penicillin should be gradually reduced; it is wrong to stop the penicillin suddenly. Koenig cautions against combining penicillin and Ectozone; he regards terramycin as unsuitable.

Color illustration 118. *Labroides dimidiatus,* cleaner wrasse, cleaning a moray eel, *Gymnothorax.* Photo by Dr. J. E. Randall.

Color illustration 119. *Hippolysmata grabhami,* cleaning shrimp, on a moray eel, *Gymnothorax.* Photo by Dr. J. E. Randall.

Color illustration 120. *Gobiosoma oceanops (Elacatinus oceanops),* cleaner gobies swimming close to a wrasse, *Thalassoma.* Photo by G. Davis.

Minor wounds of giant sea-anemones will heal in an Ectozone bath (one teaspoonful to 13 gallons of sea water).

## Fish diseases

Fish diseases tend to break out after fish have been moved. Delicate fish should be transferred in a capture bell or something similar, not in a net.

## Fungus diseases (Saprolegnia)

These appear in the form of filaments, which are often bushy. They can be treated with griseofulvin (one 250-mg. tablet in 22 gallons water). A reduction in temperature and a sudden transfer to less dense water will also help.

## Exophthalmus

This can be due to several causes: unbalanced feeding, bleeding in the head region (e.g. after a dragonfish sting), allegedly also to excess ultraviolet radiation.

## Ichthyophonus *disease*

*Ichthyophonus hoferi* is a parasitic fungus, which may infect all the internal organs of a fish and so several symptoms may appear; for example, exophthalmus, fin destruction, swollen belly, fluid in the body cavity, skin and muscle abscesses, conspicuous spotting, raised scales. This disease can be largely prevented by not feeding with the flesh of diseased fresh-water fish. In slight infections phenoxethol or para-chloro-phenoxethol is said to help, but I do not know whether this applies to sea water.

## Ichthyophthirius *disease*

The parasitic protozoan *Ichthyophthirius* forms white nodules (white spot), 1 mm. in diameter, on the fins and body. For treatment one can give trypaflavin or quinine in the water until the disease disappears. Alternatively one of these drugs can simply be painted on to the fish.

## Lymphocystis *disease*

Nodules up to over 4 mm. across, which may ulcerate, later coalesce into patches on different parts of the body. Chlupaty recommends that the infected places should be excised surgically and the wound painted with dilute iodine. Otherwise the fish should be killed immediately.

## Oodinium *disease*

This disease is caused by the dinoflagellate *Oodinium ocellatum* and is particularly common and troublesome. The parasites are quite large whitish unicellular organisms which in serious cases may form a dense covering over the whole fish. The disease can be treated by a prolonged bath (two to three days) in quinine hydrochloride (1·5 g. in 100 litres (22 gallons) water) or, depending on the size of the fish, in a short-term bath (two to twelve hours) in trypaflavin (1 g. in 100 litres water). The most commonly used remedy is a prolonged bath for five to seven days in copper sulphate solution (163 mg. $CuSO_4 \cdot 5H_2O$ in 100 litres water); according to the experience of some aquarists half this concentration is sufficient. During this treatment there should be powerful aeration, if possible with oxygen. Nevertheless, this bath is not tolerated by all fish. Algae and invertebrates, particularly sea-anemones, die in extremely low concentrations of copper, and the products of their decomposition may then quickly kill the fish. The danger of an *Oodinium* infection is particularly great in fish imported from the West Indies.

## *Obesity*

In community tanks greedy species may quite quickly become fat and sluggish. This can only be cured by fasting, although this is not always possible with old fish.

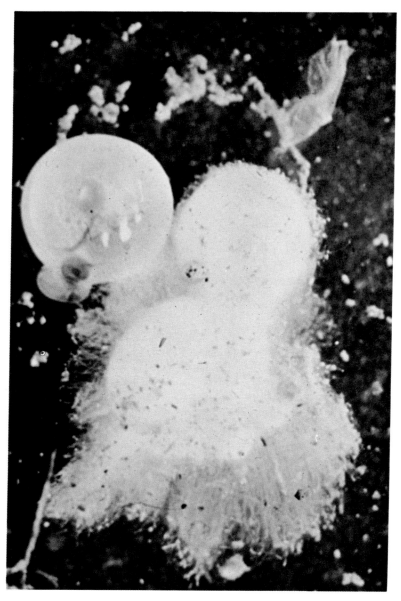

Color illustration 121. Fungused fish eggs. Photo by Frickhinger.

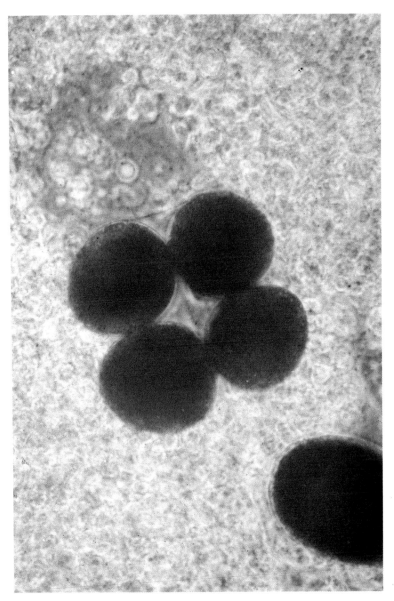

Color illustration 122. *Oodinium ocellatum.* Photo by Frickhinger.

## Nematodes

It is sometimes possible to detect clusters of nematodes (threadworms) in thin, transparent parts of the body in some fish (e.g. in the head of *Stephanolepis*). It would be best not to buy such fish.

In principle, diseased fish should be kept alone in a quarantine tank during the period of treatment.

## Additional Suggested Reading

**Marine aquarium fishes**

Allen, G. E. 1972. *The Anemonefishes, their Classification and Biology.*

Axelrod, Dr. H. R. and C. W. Emmens. 1969. *Exotic Marine Fishes.*

Axelrod, Dr. H. R. and W. E. Burgess. 1973. *Salt-water Aquarium Fish.*

Barker, C. S. 1972. *Starting a Marine Aquarium.*

Braker, W. P. and E. L. Fisher. 1966. *Marine Tropicals.*

Burgess, W. E. and Dr. H. R. Axelrod. 1972. *Pacific Marine Fishes, Book I.*

Randall, J. E. 1968. *Caribbean Reef Fishes.*

**Fish diseases**

Amlacher, E., D. A. Conroy and R. L. Herman. 1970. *Textbook of Fish Diseases.*

Reichenback-Klinke, H. 1965. *Principal Diseases of Lower Vertebrates. Book I. Diseases of Fishes.*

Sindermann, C. J. 1966. *Diseases of Marine Fishes.*

**Marine invertebrates**

Friese, U. Erich. 1972. *Sea Anemones.*

Friese, U. Erich. 1973. *Marine Invertebrates for the Home Aquarium*

These books are available from T. F. H. Publications, Inc., Box 27, Neptune City, New Jersey or at your local pet shop.

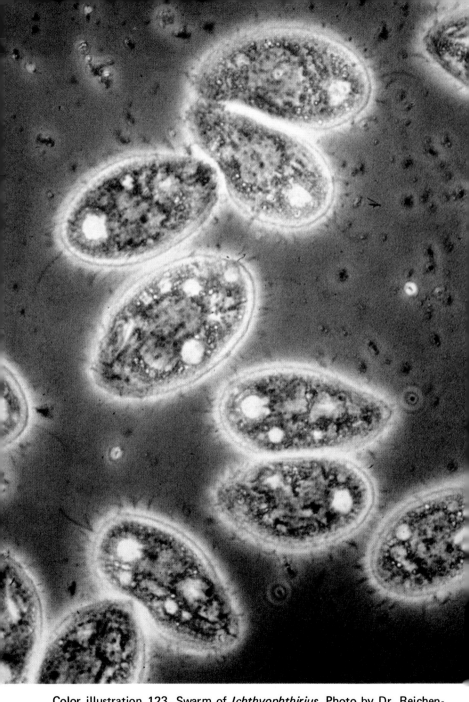

Color illustration 123. Swarm of *Ichthyophthirius*. Photo by Dr. Reichenbach-Klinke.

Color illustration 124. *Gasterosteus aculeatus,* three-spiked stickleback, with white spot disease. Photo by Dr. Reichenbach-Klinke.

Color illustration
125. A butterfly-
fish, *Chelmon,*
with exophthal-
mus. Photo by
Dr. Reichen-
bach—Klinke.

# Index

| | | | |
|---|---|---|---|
| *Abudefduf* | 68 | Blennioidea | 82–84 |
| *Acanthurus* | 74 | *Blennius* | 93 |
| *Acronurus* | 89 | *Bodianus* | 102 |
| *Acropora* | 99 | *Boleophthalmus* | 37 |
| *Actinia* | 32 | *Boops* | 51 |
| *Aeoliscus* | 99 | Boxfishes | 78 |
| Aeration | 26 | Brackish water | 9, 10 |
| *Aiptaisia* | 32 | Breeding marine fish | 92–95 |
| Algal fertilizers | 29 | Brood protection | 95, 96 |
| *Alpheus* | 99, 100 | *Bunodactis* | 32 |
| *Amanses* | 78 | Butterflyfishes | 56–60 |
| *Amphiprion* | | | |
| 14, 25, 31, 69, 70, 93, 94, 100 | | *Callianassa* | 99 |
| Anemone-fish    see *Amphiprion* | | *Callinectes* | 35 |
| *Anemonia* | 32, 97, 100 | Camouflage | 13 |
| Angelfishes, marine | 60–65 | *Canthigaster* | 81 |
| *Angelichthys* | 64, 65 | *Carcinus* | 37 |
| *Anisotremus* | 49, 102 | Cardinal fishes | 50, 51 |
| Annelid worms | 34 | *Cardium* | 33 |
| *Antennarius* | 89 | *Caulerpa* | 28, 29 |
| *Anthias* | 50 | *Centropristis* | 96 |
| *Aplysia* | 33 | *Cephalopholis* | 13, 49 |
| Apodes | 88 | Cephalopods | 33, 34 |
| *Apogon* | 14, 42, 50 | *Chaetodon* | 58–60 |
| *Arbacia* | 36 | *Chaetodontophus* | 62 |
| *Arca* | 33 | *Chelmon* | 45, 56 |
| *Arothron* | 81 | *Chilomycterus* | 79 |
| *Aspidontus* | 83, 103 | Chitons | 32 |
| | | *Chromileptis* | 50 |
| *Balistapus* | 77 | *Chromis* | 65, 66 |
| *Balistoides* | 77 | *Cirrhitichthys* | 54 |
| *Bartholomaea* | 100 | *Cladonema* | 31 |
| Batfishes | 86 | Cleaners | 101–104 |
| *Bathygobius* | 40 | Coelenterates | 31 |
| Bivalve molluscs | 33 | Coloration, general | 12, 13 |
| Blennies | 83, 84 | *Conus* | 33 |

| | |
|---|---|
| *Coris* 13, 71, 72, 90, 102 | *Gobiosoma* 85 |
| *Crenilabrus* 102 | *Gobius* 85, 100 |
| *Cristiceps* 84 | *Golfingia* 36 |
| Crustaceans 35 | *Gomphosus* 45, 90 |
| *Cryptocentrus* 99 | *Gramma* 50, 102 |
| Curlyfins 53 | *Grammistes* 49 |
| *Cyclichthys* 79 | Groupers 49–50 |
| *Cypraea* 33 | Grunts 48, 49 |
| | Gurnards 87 |
| Damselfishes 65 | |
| *Dascyllus* | *Haemulon* 13, 49 |
| 13, 25, 68, 69, 99, 100 | *Harpalocarcinus* 99 |
| *Dendrochirus* 87 | *Hemibalistes* 77 |
| Density 23 | *Heniochus* 13, 56, 102 |
| *Dentex* 51 | *Heteromysis* 100 |
| *Diadema* 99 | *Hippocampus* 19, 88, 94 |
| *Diodon* 79 | *Histrio* 89 |
| *Diplodus* 51 | *Holacanthus* 64, 101 |
| *Discosoma* 100 | *Holocentrum* 51 |
| Drums 51, 53 | |
| | *Ichthyophonus* disease 106 |
| Echinoderms 35, 36 | *Ichthyophthirius* disease 106 |
| *Ecsenius* 45, 84 | *Iniistius* 72 |
| *Elecatinus* 85, 102 | Invertebrates 30–36 |
| *Eledone* 33 | |
| *Epinephelus* 13, 49 | Jarbua 48 |
| *Eques* 51, 53 | *Junceella* 100 |
| *Eupagurus* 35 | |
| Exophthalmus 106 | King-crabs 34 |
| | |
| Fiddler-crab 37 | *Labroides* 42, 71, 102, 103 |
| Filefishes 78 | *Lactoria* 79 |
| Filtration 26, 27 | *Leander* 35 |
| *Forcipiger* 45, 58 | Leatherjackets 78 |
| Fresh water 10 | Lighting 26, 27 |
| | *Limulus* 34 |
| *Gnathypops* 84 | Lizard-fishes 85 |
| *Gobiodon* 85 | *Lophius* 89 |
| Gobioidea 84, 85 | *Lutjanus* 48 |

| | | | |
|---|---|---|---|
| *Lymphocystis* disease | 107 | *Petroscirtes* | 83 |
| *Lysmata* | 35 | Picasso Fish | 77 |
| | | Pilot Fish | 99 |
| Medusae | 31 | *Pinna* | 33 |
| *Melichthys* | 76 | Pipefishes | 88 |
| *Monodactylus* | 86 | Plants | 28, 29 |
| Moorish Idol | 60 | *Platax* | 86 |
| *Morone* | 49 | Plectognathi | 74, 76–81 |
| Mudskippers | 37, 41 | *Plectorhynchus* | 54, 56 |
| *Mullus* | 53 | *Plotosus* | 87 |
| *Murex* | 32 | *Pocillopora* | 99 |
| *Mycteroperca* | 49 | *Pomacanthodes* | 62, 63 |
| *Myripristis* | 51 | *Pomacanthus* | 63 |
| | | *Pomacentrus* | 65 |
| *Naso* | 74 | Porcupinefishes | 79 |
| *Nassa* | 33 | *Portunus* | 35 |
| *Naucrates* | 99, 102 | *Premnas* | 70 |
| Nematodes | 108 | *Pseudalutarius* | 78 |
| *Nereis* | 36 | *Pseudapocryptes* | 37 |
| | | *Pseudobalistes* | 76 |
| Octopus | see Cephalopods | *Pseudoscarus* | 42 |
| Obesity | 107 | *Pseudupeneus* | 53 |
| *Odonus* | 76 | *Pterois* | 46, 87 |
| *Oodinium* disease | 107 | Pufferfishes | 81 |
| *Opistognathus* | 84 | *Pygoplites* | 64 |
| *Ostracion* | 78, 79, 89 | | |
| *Oxyjulis* | 102 | Quarantine | 105 |
| *Paracanthurus* | 73 | Rabbitfish | 73 |
| *Paracentrotus* | 36 | Red mullets | 53 |
| *Parachaetodon* | 58, 59 | *Remora* | 102 |
| *Paracirrhites* | 54 | *Rhinecanthus* | 77 |
| *Paragobiodon* | 85 | *Roccus* | 49 |
| *Parapercis* | 85 | *Runula* | 83, 84 |
| Parrotfishes | 42, 72, 73 | | |
| *Parupeneus* | 53 | Salinity | 23 |
| Pediculati | 88 | Salts | see Sea water |
| *Periclimenes* | 100 | *Saprolegnia* | 106 |
| *Periophthalmus* | 37, 41 | *Sargus* | 51 |

| | | | | |
|---|---|---|---|---|
| *Scarus* | 42, 73 | *Stoichactis* | | 31, 100 |
| *Scorpaena* | 13, 46, 86 | *Sufflamen* | | 77 |
| *Scorpaenopsis* | 86 | Surfperches | | 96 |
| Scorpion-fishes | 86 | Surgeonfish | | 73, 74 |
| Sea-bream | 51 | Sweetlips | | 54 |
| Sea-horses | 15–20, 88 | *Synanceja* | | 87 |
| Sea water | 9, 10, 21–23 | *Syngnathus* | | 88 |
| *Sebastes* | 86 | | | |
| *Serranellus* | 49, 96 | Tanks | | 23, 24 |
| *Serranus* | 49 | *Tetrosomus* | | 79 |
| *Sertularia* | 31 | *Thalassoma* | 42, 72, 90, | 100, 102 |
| *Siganus* | 73 | *Therapon* | | 48 |
| Silverfishes | 86 | *Tholichthys* | | 89 |
| *Siphamia* | 51 | *Tridacna* | | 97 |
| Snails | 32, 33 | Triggerfishes | | 76 |
| Snappers | 48 | *Tripterygion* | | 84 |
| Soldier Fishes | 51 | *Tubularia* | | 31 |
| *Sparisoma* | 43, 73 | *Typhlogobius* | | 99 |
| *Sphaeroides* | 81 | | | |
| Spikefishes | 76 | *Uca* | | 37 |
| Spinefeet | 73 | *Upeneus* | | 53 |
| *Spirographis* | 34 | | | |
| Sponges | 31 | Wrasse | | 71, 72 |
| Squirrelfishes | 51 | | | |
| *Stenopus* | 35, 101 | *Xiphosura* | see King-crabs | |
| *Stenorhynchus* | 100 | | | |
| *Stephanolepis* | 78 | *Zanclus* | | 45, 60 |
| *Stethojulis* | 90 | *Zebrasoma* | | 74 |